*'The book is a sort of alarm clock,
calling the reader to faith and prayer'*
The Ampleforth Journal

*'Bracing like a dip in the sea
but also very comforting'*
Association of Catholic Women

*'It cuts through much current confusion,
including that over chastity and marriage'*
Ambrose, Bishop of Hexham & Newcastle

*'Admirable as an expression of a layman's views
and deeply held faith which he wants to communicate
strongly and share by many ingenious means.'*
A Jesuit priest

*'I am so pleased to have a copy of this book
I keep it beside me and refer to it constantly
as a guide and comfort.'*
A fellow layman

'I should like to give Wake up to God
*to every God-parent as a reminder
of the responsibility they have solemnly undertaken.'*
A mother of four young children

**The book carries the *Imprimatur* and *Nihil obstat*.
They are a declaration that it is free from doctrinal or moral
error and so conforms to the true teaching of
the Church.**

Cover illustration from the original painting
by Mary de Piro:
The Power of Pentecost
See the Sequence on page 67

First edition: JANUARY 1996
Revised and reprinted in June 1997
Enlarged and reprinted with the
OMEGA Work-out added in August 1998
Enlarged and reprinted in September 1999
Reprinted 2000, 2001, 2002, 2003, 2004, 2005, 2006,
2007 (twice) 2008 and 2009
Copyright ©: J. M. REID 1995

IMPRIMATUR
Bishop M. Ambrose DD DCL
Bishop of Coimbatore
Coimbatore
India
26 July 1995

NIHIL OBSTAT
Censor Deputatus
Fr Antony Packiasamy
Rector
Good Shepherd Seminary
Coimbatore
India

Published by:

Book Disciples,
7 Bradbourne Street,
London SW6 3TF
Great Britain

Printed by: St Joseph's Press, Thiruvananthapuram, Kerala, India

ISBN 0 9526612 0 9

WAKE UP TO GOD

J. M. Reid

A BOOK DISCIPLE
LONDON

From the fourth edition, dedicated to my friend
George Basil Hume (1923-99),
Order of St. Benedict, Cardinal, Order of Merit,
Abbot of Ampleforth, Archbishop of Westminister,
He chose this passage to be read at his funeral:

'All men who were ignorant of God were foolish by nature;
and they were unable by the good things that are seen
                                       to know Him who exists.
nor did they recognise the craftsman while paying heed to His works;
but they supposed that either fire or wind or swift air,
or the circle of the stars, or turbulent water,
or the luminaries of heaven were the gods that rule the world.

If through delight in the beauty of these things
men assumed them to be gods,
let them know how much better than those is their Lord;
for the author of beauty created them.
And if men were amazed at their power and working,
let them perceive from them
how much more powerful is He who formed them.
For from the greatness and beauty of created things
comes a corresponding perception of their Creator.

Yet these men are little to be blamed,
for perhaps they go astray while seeking God and
                                       desiring to find Him.
For us they live among His works they keep searching,
and they trust in what they see,
because the things that are seen are beautiful.

Yet again, not even they are to be excused;
for if they had the power to know so much
that they could investigate the world,
how did they fail to find sooner the Lord of these things?'
                                       (Book of Wisdom 13:1-9)

Spiritual Communion

'A Spiritual Communion acts on the soul as blowing does on a cinder-covered fire which was about to go out. Whenever you feel your love of God growing cold, quickly make a Spiritual Communion.' Curé d' Ars

Refer also to St Alphonso de Liguori, St Catherine of Sienna, St Margaret Mary Alacoque and St Thomas Aquinas.
St Bernardette and St Francis de Sales made a Spiritual Communion regularly and often during the day and night.

Whenever you are unable to receive Our Lord sacramentally, you ask Him to come to you spiritually and His Grace will increase in you. It is a wonderful way of acknowledging your dependence on Him. "Ask and you shall receive".

'Lord I am not worthy that
 Thou shouldst enter under my roof,
  but only say the word
   and my soul shall be healed.'
(An indulgence of 500 days if thrice repeated)

'O Jesus I turn towards the Holy Tabernacle where Thou livest hidden for love of me. I love Thee, O my God. I cannot receive Thee in Holy Communion. Come nevertheless and visit me with Thy Grace. Come spiritually into my heart. Purify it. Sanctify it. Render it like unto Thine own.'

☖

If you practise the holy exercise of Spiritual Communion several times each day, within a month you will see your heart completely changed.' St Leonard Port Maurice

'Abide in Me and I in you.' (John 15:4)

I, John Reid, beseech Thee

O God, from my youth Thou hast taught me;
unto old age and grey hairs, forsake me not
till I proclaim Thee to all the generations to come.
(Psalm 70:17–18)

Remember me, O Lord that rulest over all power,
creator and sustainer of all life;
command well-ordered words from my pen
that they may be pleasing to Thee

✠

Especially I remember

'We are not allowed neutrality when faced with the question of God.
We can only say yes or no, and this with all the consequences
extending right down to the smallest details of life.'
To Look on Christ Cardinal Joseph Ratzinger

'Jesus Christ is the Truth to be told,
the Way to be walked,
the light to be lit.'
Mother Teresa of Calcutta

'Woe to humanity which loses the sense of truth,
the courage to seek it,
and the trust to find it.
Not only faith would be compromised by this
but also the very meaning of life'
Pope John Paul II (1998)

[Table of Contents Pages 167 & 168]

Preface

This little book is thought of by its author, a layman, as a 'primer', a word deliberately selected for its several meanings. The first: an introduction and guide to the study of a subject. I emphasise, however, that it is not comprehensive but selective, reflecting a personal Faith with its imperfections and failings. A primer is also an undercoat; a finish has to be applied over it. Two other senses of the word appear later.

My subject is the value and meaning of human life. This has to be seen again as it was created, for life began, continues and ends in God. Natural life must be lifted up again to the supernatural. For a Christian this translates to winning personal salvation for a life of eternal happiness – or failing to do so as a result of self-condemnation and going to Hell, a real, terrifying possibility.

Personal salvation depends on belief in God and the doing of His Word. This may be likened to wearing a protective cloak, a seamless garment for the soul. It is knitted, the stitches being the teaching of God's Church. If any stitch is broken by disobedience and is not immediately repaired, the garment gapes, leaving the soul exposed to injury which could be mortal to its eternal life.

This cloak is not a garment always found comfortable to wear, but that is a small price to pay for the protection and safe passage promised. It is precious and should be preserved at all costs. The material wears thin, holes torn in it enlarge; being knitted, there is the risk of its unravelling completely. Constant reinforcement and running repairs are essential to ensure that it lasts the whole journey.

As well as being a protective cloak, God's Word can be seen as a chain handrail, connected links running the length of the path

PREFACE

to be taken from conception and birth to death and the hereafter, secured at both ends. Given access to it at Baptism, it can be firmly grasped throughout the journey to prevent a fall from the path into the abyss running alongside. At the end of the chain stands our loving Creator, to be met with face to face.

Primer also means 'a devotional manual for the laity': there is at least one prayer per chapter.

A list of books is added and some web resources. Few of us have studied metaphysics (a branch of philosophy dealing with the nature of existence, truth and knowledge) or extended our religious knowledge since we left school. We are strongly tempted to see life pretty much as most people around us see it, people who may no longer acknowledge God and think purely in secular, permissive terms; people who are inclined to believe that death is a return to nothingness. Are we challenging this view?

Finally, all true Christians have been given a guarantee.* We have only to practise our declared belief, seeking the Truth and, especially, yielding our 'self' to it, and an immortal future in Paradise is assured. This guarantee is available to every faithful believer in Christ.

Enough: let us get on, time is limited. To forfeit the happiness of the love of God for all eternity because we did not find out before it was too late just how to secure that reward, is a risk no one can afford to take.

Wake up to God and with Him at the end.

J. M. Reid, London, 1995
Nunc dimittis servum tuum, Domine ... (Luke 2:29)

---
* Christ's guarantee:

Jesus said: 'Truly, truly, I say to you, he who hears My Word and believes Him Who sent Me, has Eternal Life' (John 5:24). Every guarantee has its small print but Jesus has writ large: 'If any man would come after Me, let him deny himself and take up his cross and follow Me. For whoever would save his life will lose it, and whoever loses his life for My sake will find it. For what will it profit a man if he gains the whole world and forfeits his (Eternal) Life?' (Matthew 16:24–6).

Opening Prayer

' I adore Thee and thank Thee, Almighty Father, for so loving us as to send Thy Son as man to redeem us, to give us life and the light of Truth. Never let me prefer sin or any dazzling worldly attraction to Thee, to the life of grace within me.

'O Lord Jesus Christ, help me to use my intellectual gifts to seek out and fight for the truth. Show me where the ideas prevailing all around me are wrong, where I must differ from the popular views and take my stand with Thee. Grant me to understand how I must live by Faith and not by material considerations, of what it means to believe in Thee and have eternal life.

'Come Holy Spirit, fill my heart and kindle in me the fire of Thy love. Inspire me to use prayer and the Sacraments to sanctify my soul and so to join the angels and saints in Heaven. *In manus tuas, Domine, commendo spiritum meum.*'

☩

'Therefore God has highly exalted Him and bestowed on Him the name which is above every name, that at the name of Jesus every knee should bow, in Heaven and on earth, and every tongue confess that Jesus Christ is Lord, to the glory of God the Father' (Philippians 2:9–11).

As commanded by Pope Gregory X in 1274, I was taught as a child always to bow my head when I uttered or heard or read the name of Jesus. (Is this still common practice?) It is a gesture of reverence and love that is commended to every reader of this book. Let it be a lifelong habit.

Three readings:

'Blessed is that simplicity which leaves
the difficult paths of questionings
and goes on in the plain and sure paths
of God's commandments.
It is faith and an upright life
that are required of you,
not the loftiness of intellect,
nor diving deep into the mysteries of God.'

The perfect victory is to triumph over one's self.
For whosoever keepeth himself in subjection,
so that sensuality obeyeth reason,
and reason in all things is obedient to Me,
he is indeed a conqueror of himself, and lord of the world'.

'Know for certain
that you must lead a dying life;
and the more a man dieth to himself,
the more doth he begin to live with God.'

The Imitation of Christ, Thomas à Kempis (See page 130)

Invocations:
'Remind us, O Lord, of our obligations, not only to each other but also to God through His Church.'
'O God, be merciful to me a sinner.'*
'The Lord reigns; let the earth rejoice!'

---
* Indulgence of 500 days. Plenary, under the usual conditions, if recited daily during a month (See page 85.)

Purpose

To achieve startling impact, the news makes headlines of eye-catching detail, focuses on contentious extracts from a speech, report or publication and presents partial interpretations of selected events. Such 'sound-bite' reporting and its counterpart 'spin' often distort the facts or masks the full context, be it an announcement, purport, picture or happening. The whole truth may be hidden, even deliberately buried; we have to accept what we are told.

Have we not become the kind of people who have evolved to want what we are given? Are we aware how much our freedom of choice has been eroded? For instance, what is mass advertising trying to do to us in brief slots on television?

Regrettably, large numbers of people now think in the bite sizes pioneered by the media. In particular, many of us have become buffet Catholics, helping ourselves only to what teaching we like, or approve, or that suits us – in bite sizes. Even worse, we have begun to reject what we dislike or find uncomfortable. (Heresy derives from the Greek word 'hairesis' which means 'choice'.) Thus we may be 'I say my prayers' Catholics but choose not to attend Holy Mass on Sundays; or we may reject the existence of Hell, no longer distinguishing mortal sin or subjectively taking a benign view of grave wrongdoing; yet we still claim to be Catholics.

Particularly common is dedication only to material contentment, improving one's own lot and that of the victims of poverty, disease and war – a political agenda rather than heeding man's overriding priority: seeking and doing the Will of God. It is man's responsibility to save his own soul and it is his duty to try to save the souls of others too. **As Pope John Paul II states clearly in *'Veritatis Splendor'*, 'Christ does not wish to put love of neighbour higher than God or to set it apart from God.'**

In short, there is in Catholic men and women today a widespread relativist, or subjective, or autonomous element, called 'own conscience', 'personal choice' or 'control of one's life', supporting an own code of conduct, an own set of values, which has taken the place of respect for, and being obedient to, God's law, the teaching of His one Holy, Catholic and Apostolic Church. The search for Truth has lost momentum or lapsed altogether.

To quote *'Veritatis Splendor'* again: 'A new situation has come about within the Christian community itself. It is no longer a matter of occasional dissent, but of an overall and systematic calling into question of traditional moral doctrine. The very foundations of moral theology are being undermined.' The Pope was addressing bishops throughout the world. His predecessor, Pope Paul VI, had put it another way. He said that the 'smoke of Satan' was in the Church.

In an attempt to combat this situation and reinforce my own Faith, I am setting down some of the essential tenets which I learnt as a boy at Ampleforth (1934–42), the casting-on stitches for my seamless knitted cloak. I shall present short sections of the chain of linked teaching in their God-embracing contexts. Especially, I hope that the teaching on particularly contested issues, contraception, for example, will be seen to fit naturally, be integral and easily acceptable. Changing the metaphor, my objective is to lay out in a rational way many of the essential ingredients of the Catholic Faith, all of them authenticated, to which the yeast of recommended reading can be added as leaven to make, with God's liberal grace, a fulfilling and soul-saving recipe. Additionally, since no such recipe will be effective unless we pray, I have supplied a prayer with each chapter. (Prayer is the subject of Chapter 5.)

1 PURPOSE

Let us then begin with a prayer breathed to the Holy Spirit for guidance:

'Come, Holy Spirit, fill the hearts of Thy faithful and kindle in them the fire of Thy love. Send forth Thy Spirit and they shall be created.'

℞ And Thou shalt renew the face of the earth.

'Let us pray: O God Who taught the hearts of the faithful by the light of Thy Holy Spirit, grant that by the gift of the same Spirit we may always be truly wise and ever rejoice in His consolation. Through Christ our Lord. Amen.'

–This prayer was said at school assembly every morning in the Big Passage at Ampleforth, led by the Headmaster, the great Fr Paul Nevill, 1924-54, or in his absence by the School Head Monitor.
– Incidentally I shall throughout use the singular second-person pronoun when referring to God, always with a capital letter. This is an ancient tradition, a distinctive, reverential and loving reference to Him Who is our Creator and our all. It is also the correct translation of the Latin, the language of the Church.

✠

The short passages in bold type in the book are sound bites to catch or focus attention within a chapter, or to prompt meditation or further study of what they really mean.

People are passionately concerned to anticipate tomorrow's big events, reflected in media speculation on the basis of information from 'reliable sources'. Compare the lack of interest in the climactic event in everyone's tomorrow, death.

Why is eschatology* of such small concern?

---
*Eschatology is the theology of death and final destiny.

2

Is There a God?

What do we mean by God? How do we imagine God? Does the existence of God depend on us or do we depend on God? Shall we meet God when we die? How should we feel if we were to meet God? Has anyone on earth seen God? Does God exist?

While it is possible to arrive at the existence of God through reason, most of us would not find it easy. Let us, then, settle for a simple, willed declaration of Faith: 'I believe in God'. Until the mid-eighteenth century, had not most people on earth believed in a god or gods and worshipped him, her, it or them? A declaration of belief, therefore, sits easily. We can be sure that God will duly reveal Himself to us, a personal God, who is real, a living God.

Christ, Who is God, is acknowledged by all Christians at their Baptism or Christening. The babies are welcomed into the Christian community, washed clean of sin and have Godparents appointed to assist their parents to bring them up as devout Christians.

Baptism bestows on Catholics the gift of Faith. It is a gift that will never leave them – although they can choose to ignore it. With a small f, faith means belief and trust – in people, things and ideas; no one could survive without it. With a capital F, it means belief and trust in God. It is worth treasuring Faith if only because, as Blaise Pascal declared in his well-known wager, we have nothing to lose if it turns out that God does not exist (see Pascal's *Pensées*).

Cardinal Basil Hume, a contemporary at Ampleforth, has been more positive: 'The eyes of Faith enable us to see, beyond the limitation of our minds and senses, that Reality which explains all things which is God.'

2 IS THERE A GOD?

We need to make a firm resolution to study how we might explain God and eternal life, not only to ourselves to our complete satisfaction but to someone who does not believe in Him; to explain, also, that this unbelief cannot be true or reasonable.

It is the solemn teaching of the Catholic Church that the existence of God *(utrum sit Deus)* can be arrived at by a process of philosophical reasoning. Vatican II confirmed this in *Dei Verbum:* 'God, the beginning and end of all things, can be known with certainty from created reality by the light of human reason.' It went on to state that through divine revelation 'those religious truths which are accessible to human reason can be known by all men with ease, with solid certitude, and with no trace of error, even in the present state of the human race' (cf. Romans 1:19–23).

In bite size, what is the answer given to our question 'Is there a God'? It is prudent to accept the existence of God until we can definitely prove otherwise. Belief demands that we get to know Him with certainty and act as He commanded.

'I believe; help Thou my unbelief' (Mark 9:24).

'God, if Thou dost exist, make me know Thee.'

✠

Baptism or Christening is still part of the social fabric. Babies are proudly taken to church; on their behalf, Christ is acknowledged; symbolically they are washed clean with water; they are made Christians and Godparents accept the responsibility of keeping their charges on the Christian path. The role of Godparent is especially important but, sadly, it is no longer undertaken as conscientiously as demanded and frequently diminishes to merely a social relationship. Such is the descent to secularism. How long before a purely civil ceremony? (Introduced in December 2000)

3

Creation, Fall and Redemption

As related in the Bible, most of us having learnt the story as children, the first man was created and human life began in the Garden of Eden. He was created by God. What God has created, He sustains; nothing exists unless kept in being by Him all the time.

We are made of nothing and it is God who continues to hold us in existence, even after death.

God is infinite: all-powerful, all-knowing, all-loving. He created a man, a person in His own image and likeness, a soul with a body and, in particular, intellect and free will. He placed this man on earth with its air, sea and land, plants, fishes, birds and animals, under the vault of the sky with its sun, planets, stars and other astral bodies, the earth that He had made for man (Genesis 1).

God gave that first man, Adam, a woman companion, Eve, and enjoined them both to obey one rule: not to eat of the tree of knowledge (Genesis 2:16–17). Alas, He was immediately defied. These two, the human race, beguiled by Lucifer, committed the first sin, Original Sin, and fell out of sanctifying grace. Thus their souls no longer remained at one with God and they committed themselves to die (Genesis 2:15–17). The Devil had made his first conquests.

Man had denied his dependence on his Creator, set himself up as an absolute in revolt against God and condemned himself (*Catechism of the Catholic Church*: 396–400). This is taught, also, by all Christian churches.

What did God do? All-merciful, He chose to heal the breach. Mankind was redeemed from Original Sin by His Son Jesus Christ through His death on the Cross. This took place only a few less than

3 CREATION, FALL AND REDEMPTION

two thousand years ago on Calvary, a hill outside Jerusalem in Israel. Then Jesus Christ rose from the tomb on the third day and after forty days, He ascended into heaven to His Father (see the four Gospels). Our salvation had been guaranteed, but only if we sought God's grace and joined our will to His.

To enable us to do this He founded His Church and sent the Third Person of the Trinity, the Holy Spirit, to direct it unerringly until the consummation of the world.

Let us pause to think about the Creation, Fall and Redemption of man. Draw some mental pictures. The mind likes pictures to savour and to assist recall. Many have been put on canvas to give us a rich artistic heritage. In particular, pictures are a great help in mental prayer.

Mental prayer is something we all engage in to a greater or lesser extent, although it may not always be related to God. We have been given the ability to think and we use this wonderful and powerful faculty to reason, to weigh, to imagine, to wish and of course to pray. We also have a huge capacity to remember. This is a function we often choose to deny when it suits our convenience. 'I forgot' is the most common excuse – and lie – in the world.

Remember now how far we have come, short though it may be. Do we really understand and grasp firmly, **that if God did not love and sustain us, we would not exist?** He created us from nothing; we are entirely in His hands and owe everything to Him; we cannot do anything without Him; we are nothing without Him. Our complete dependence on God has fundamental implications for us which cannot be ignored and must never be forgotten.

Moreover, it is impossible intelligently to handle anything at all – including one's own self – without knowing the purpose for which it was made; so what are my Maker's instructions? (See Chapter 7)

17

A Prayer of Thanksgiving:

'I give Thee thanks, O Lord, for all the benefits which Thou hast granted me, and especially for having protected me so mercifully during this day (night).'

– This is a prayer that might be said every morning and evening to thank our loving Creator for the life He has given us, and for everything else in our life. It comes from the Ampleforth Prayer Book which all us boys used daily.

– To provide a choice, here is another:

'I thank Thee, Almighty God, for having granted me all these years of life, and I ask Thy pardon for not having served Thee better, as Thou deserved and as was my duty. I offer Thee my joys, sufferings, thoughts and actions during this day (night) in reparation for the Passion and Crucifixion of Thy Son, Jesus Christ. Watch over me and guide me through Thy Holy Spirit. Amen.'

– Or compose one for yourself.

✠

'Oh, it was a sight fitted to stir the soul of man to its profoundest depths, and, if he owned a heart at all, to lift that heart in adoration and gratitude to the great Creator of this magnificent and glorious universe!'

From *The Coral Island:* R. M. Ballantine (1825–94), a Scottish writer of adventure tales for boys, including this novel of exhilarating freedom and excitement.

When last saw you such a sight? Did you thank God?

4
What about Evolution?

An objective of this book is to seed the mind with questions, to prompt re-examination and study, in order to arrive at answers which can be defended with confidence. Evolution is a subject in our context particularly suited to this exercise.

An immediate response to the question posed might be: do not let it be a distraction; our concern should be not with how man originated but why, and with what man is. Nevertheless the topic, which has far-reaching implications for mankind, regularly hits the news and deserves discussion.

The theory of evolution sounds plausible and has great appeal. Briefly explained, it is the progressive evolvement of new species from an unknown origin via primitive organisms, fishes, birds and animals, up to the emergence of man. For a Christian such evolution must start from a created beginning of matter and time; moreover, an ape with responsive instincts cannot evolve into a man with a soul, intellect and free will. A Christian believes in God and that God made man, a person in His own image and likeness with a soul. Although he shares their physical features, man is distinct from the great apes and is not an animal.

If God had so wished, He could have created the world and its creatures by evolutionary means. Then he could have changed an ape-like animal into a man with a soul, who further evolved into the man and woman we know today. Such a creative process would not necessarily conflict with the story in Genesis. On the other hand, God could just as easily have made the world in six days as recounted in Genesis. He is Almighty God.

Let us boldly look at the evidence against evolution. It is acknowledged to this day that there has never been a confirmed example of one species evolving into another, as distinct from developments within a species. And why should evolution occur anyway? In particular, there is no incontrovertible evidence that any ape-like animal species evolved into a human being, hard though many have tried to persuade people to accept the Darwinian atheistic hypothesis on the basis of bits of fossils and animal remains, numerous fakes including one that was even accepted by a thinker such as Teilhard de Chardin, drawings of imagined manlike creatures, and conjuring up immeasurable millions of years essential to the credibility of the theory. Further, evolution will not just have stopped: so what is man now evolving into, and are there any signs of progress?

The evolutionists are demonstrably wilful thinkers, making assumptions to fit their theories. They are unquenchable optimists. Procrustean by nature: wherever the evidence they need is proved false or not supportive, they are undeterred, prisoners of a myth and frequently practising tautology. Even Darwin had his doubts about evolution. He also admitted that geological evidence did not support his theory. Subsequently, others have replaced it with neo-Darwinism, based on random genetic mutations and natural selection. The validity of both depends on the age of the earth. Is it millions of years old or only thousands? How can we know? There are conflicting claims. Scientists with their techniques and instruments could not agree on the age of the Turin Shroud, not older than two thousand years; are they any more reliable looking at a fossil or a piece of bone where the claimed age is millions of years?

Let me throw two facts into the ring. No one has ever observed a spontaneous, inheritable, viable genetic mutation that has resulted in a changed physical characteristic. Moreover, there is a well-known natural barrier in genetic development: genetic

4 WHAT ABOUT EVOLUTION?

homeostasis. Second, in spite of the existence of millions of fossils, no one has ever produced a sequence of them showing progressive evolutionary change.

Most of us who have had the theory of evolution dictated to us do not understand it in detail, neither Darwinism nor neo-Darwinism, but have had no reason to challenge it. After all, is it not widely accepted at the highest scientific levels? Who is not familiar with the tree of life, illustrating the evolution of animal life from earliest times down to some fearsome hairy bipeds portrayed as our early ancestors?

Could the tree of life be an imaginative invention? It is a fact that the equally well-known geological column was transformed from an illustration of rock strata to a representation of ages related to the rock strata, this without any foundation whatsoever.

Is the theory of evolution the greatest confidence trick in the history of the world, as some eminent scientists now claim? In that event, what would be the effect on how millions view the destiny of the human race and on its belief in God? From his beginning has not man shown an overwhelming desire to be autonomous, independent of nature, accountable only to himself? Moreover, has he not proved as a result to be the great destroyer of all aspects of his natural environment?

Evolution: what an important and fascinating subject for study! No doubt you will be astonished at the temerity of an attempt to discredit the theory of evolution. Good. But do not just reject it: study the subject and find facts to defeat it. Start with Darwin's *Origin of the Species*. (If it happens to be the Everyman Library Centenary Edition – J. M. Dent & Sons, London 1956 – note what Professor Thompson FRS has to say in his Introduction.) Two books are recommended in the Book List: page 163

Before moving on, I shall try further to encourage exploration of the subject by adding that we human beings can and do delude ourselves very easily and are ready subjects for self-deception. Moreover, having to acknowledge a Supreme Being, our Loving Creator, Who also sustains us, has far-reaching implications and diminishes our large egos. Scientists, especially, welcome the theory of evolution: it is intriguing and difficult to dispute; they feel comfortable with it and it provides a welcome livelihood. Opposition within their ranks is strongly – and often unfairly – resisted by the majority. The truth, however, is not always what a majority decides. What spectacular confusion the overthrow of Darwinism would cause!

As stated at the beginning of this chapter, one of this book's objectives is to urge research and study, always accompanied by prayer. Hence a challenge against the theory of evolution has been thrown down: do try to determine its validity.

A last word : it is an article of the Creed that God Almighty is the Creator of Heaven and earth.

And now, especially those who have not had contact with the language since school, somehow (with a dictionary from the local library? a friend?), translate this French verse into English.

>Je suis la Lumière
>Et vous ne Me voyez pas;
>Je suis la Route,
>Et vous ne Me suivez pas;
>Je suis la Vérité
>Et vous ne Me croyez pas;
>Je suis la Vie
>Et vous ne Me cherchez pas;
>Je suis votre Chef
>Et vous ne M'obéissez pas;
>Je suis votre Dieu
>Et vous ne Me priez pas;
>>Si vous êtes malheureux
>>Ne Me le reprochez pas.

– A little research exercise, and listen to God's words.

5

Prayer

My book is studded with prayers because they are the only means of asking for the grace our souls need to live in the love of God. 'Help me to accept, dear Jesus,' as did St Augustine, 'that Thou hast made us, O Lord, for Thyself, and our heart shall find no rest till it rests in Thee.' Living and praying should become synonymous. Indeed each one of us can become a saint if we really desire it; we just ask God for the grace to do it and apply ourselves wholeheartedly and humbly. If we fail it will not be His fault.

Who wants to become a saint? If we believe that God made us, that life on earth is but a journey to a life with Him, our Eternal Creator, is not our best course to please Him as much as we can, to do His Will? That is all being a saint means. We devote to Him the comparatively short time of our life on earth for the sake of spending an eternity of happiness in His loving arms. To achieve this we must pray and listen to Him.

Even those who do not believe in God find themselves saying a prayer: in moments of stress or danger; in need of urgent help; when desperate or in fear of the unknown. They are moved to do so by the unquenchable spirit in their weak, mortal self, a spirit that will never die and which is their immortal soul.

To pray is to raise the mind and heart to God. To pray is to talk to God, to look into His countenance, to contemplate Him and to listen to Him. This can be done directly or with the help of His special friends, His saints. In particular, He listens to His Blessed Mother, the Virgin Mary. Remember, she is our Mother too.

More than any of my dear ones, relatives or friends, He who created me is always beside me, loving me, sustaining me, wishing me well. He is always ready with all the help I need; I have only to ask Him: 'May the Lord overwhelm me with His grace.' Indeed He wants me to place myself entirely in His loving hands and allow Him to guide me through my life to Him.

It is not in spite of my unworthiness but because of it that God, who loves each one of us, seeks my love.

How can any of us resist not constantly seeking Him out to talk to and ask His advice? Do you remember the admonition at the end of that French verse in the previous chapter?

'Lord, I shall be very busy this day; if I forget Thee, do not Thou forget me.'

Sir Jacob Astley, English soldier and royalist, 1579–1652, before a battle.

- None of us, however, is so busy as not to be able to say a simple prayer, like grace before a meal, for example:
  'Bless us, O Lord, and these Thy gifts which we are about to receive from Thy bounty, through Christ our Lord.'
- And after:
  'We give Thee thanks, Almighty God, for all the benefits we have received, Who lives and reigns for ever. Amen.'
- Then add:
  'May the souls of the faithful departed', making the Sign of the Cross ✠, 'through the mercy of God, rest in peace. Amen.'
- Another prayer once commonly said three times a day, at dawn, noon and sunset, when the church bell was rung as a reminder, is the *'Angelus'*:
  ℣ The Angel of the Lord declared unto Mary
  ℟ And she conceived of the Holy Spirit

℣ Hail Mary, full of grace, the Lord is with thee: blessed art thou among women, and blessed is the fruit of thy womb, Jesus. Holy Mary, Mother of God, pray for us sinners, now, and at the hour of our death. Amen.
℣ Behold the handmaid of the Lord
℟ Be it done to me according to thy word
Hail Mary...
℣ And the Word was made Flesh
℟ And dwelt amongst us
Hail Mary...
℣ Pray for us, O Holy Mother of God
℟ That we may be made worthy of the promises of Christ.
'Let us pray:
Pour forth, we beseech Thee, O Lord, Thy grace into our hearts, that we, to whom the Incarnation of Christ, Thy Son, was made known by the message of an angel, may be brought by His Passion and Cross ✠ to the glory of His Resurrection, through the same Christ our Lord. Amen. ✠ May the souls of the faithful departed, through the mercy of God, rest in peace. Amen.'
– A watch which can be set to alert the wearer at the appropriate times can take the place of the ringing of the church bell.

✠

The prayers selected in my book are proven exercises for keeping spiritually fit. There are, however, many others which we can look for and choose from, and all can contribute to helping us compose our own prayers, short or long, which will appeal to our loving Father that much more.

Most of us take some exercise every day – or we are advised to – to keep physically fit. Are we giving the same attention to spiritual health? Our bodies will grow old and creaky and die, but our souls have an everlasting life. How do we want them to spend it?

Finally, remember that no prayer which is subject to God's Will ever goes unanswered. We must never be discouraged; we have to be patient. Since we usually want our prayer to be answered 'now', we have to remember that now has no meaning in Eternity. Also, **it is not what we want but what God wants for us in His love and mercy that He will certainly grant in response to prayer.** Our prayer must reflect this trust in Him.

Meditation can be of signal benefit to everyone. It is particularly important to prayer life. A man of great holiness has left us an example of how he meditated:

'God has created me to do Him some definite service; He has committed some work to me which He has not committed to another. I am a link in a chain, a bond of connection between persons. He has not created me for nought. I shall do good, I shall do His work. I shall be an angel of peace, a preacher of truth in my own place while not intending it – if I do but keep His Commandments.

'Then I will trust Him. Whatever, wherever I am, I can never be thrown away. If I am in sickness, my sickness may serve Him; if I am in sorrow my sorrow may serve Him. He does nothing in vain. He knows what He is about. He may take away my friends. He may throw me among strangers. He may make me feel desolate, make my spirit sink, hide my future from me – still He knows what He is about.'

John Henry, Cardinal Newman

Finally, here is a motto taught by the Benedictines:
Laborare est orare. (To work is to pray.) Think about it.
I conclude this chapter with Padre Pio's famous maxim: "Pray, hope and don't worry."

The Bible

We now turn to the Bible, a source of many prayers and of which Genesis, referred to in Chapter 2, is the first book.

In truth, the first five books, the Pentateuch, are traditionally ascribed to Moses. They are commonly known as Genesis, Exodus, Leviticus, Numbers and Deuteronomy.

What is the Bible? It is the world's most published book. It has been translated into more languages than any other. It is the most studied and researched. It is the most read and the most quoted. Quite a reputation! Ask yourself why.

The Bible contains divinely revealed realities committed to writing under the inspiration of the Holy Spirit. The Christian Church regards them as sacred and canonical, written by men chosen by God to set down what He wanted (see *'Dogmatic Constitution on Divine Revelation'*, Vatican II). The Books of Scripture must be acknowledged as teaching firmly, faithfully and without error that truth which God wanted put into sacred writing for the sake of our salvation (*ibid.*).

The Bible comprises the Old and the New Testaments. Both parts are history, a record of past events, and the Old Testament is rich in other reading. It is worth repeating that all Christians accept that both parts were inspired by God and are, therefore, authoritative. The Christian Church accepts the Bible, whole and entire, as sacred and canonical, written under the direction of the Holy Spirit (cf. John 20:31; 2 Timothy 3:16–17; 2 Peter 1:19–21).

The first eleven chapters of the Book of Genesis prove that, left to ourselves without the grace and guidance of God, we are defective (liable to fail) and do our worst. This has applied throughout history since the Fall and is doing so today. The second part shows how God began to rescue us by creating a people of God. The whole Book of Genesis points to the coming of Christ and the mission of the Church He will found.

How many of us have read the Bible? Or the Old Testament? The New Testament, then? Or even just one of the Gospels?

Expert guidance on how to read the Bible is given in the Book List. (page 159).

(I happened to write 46 chapters; the Bible has 46 books!)

The meaning, direction and right conduct of every human life is there in the life of Jesus as revealed in the Gospels and interpreted by His Church. It is the duty of every Christian to accept this and to make it known to anyone not fortunate enough to have been so taught, as well as to whomsoever may since have rejected the teaching they received. Such a duty is required because of one's being a baptised, practising member of the one, Holy, Catholic and Apostolic Church. As already stated (Chapter 2), the gift of Faith is bestowed at Baptism; rejection of that gift puts the soul in mortal peril. We must not allow the supernatural life received at Baptism to die. Even worse, we must not kill it.

One of the rubrics at Baptism is the putting of a white garment on the baby receiving the Sacrament. Usually a shawl (a sort of seamless cloak?), it is a symbol of innocence and protection. May it always signal a period of childhood during which the child is at peace to find its feet, to learn the difference between right and wrong and to develop a sense of values and responsibility. **Parents have a duty to teach their children the fundamental laws of right and wrong.**

'Woe to the world for temptations to sin,' said Jesus (Matthew 18:7). The dire warning He went on to give (verses 8–9) repeated what He said in His Sermon on the Mount. We cannot dismiss or ignore it, particularly since we know how much

He loves us. Like Him we love our children: do we ensure that they too know His warning?

The following prayer will remind parents and Godparents of their undertaking at Baptism expressed in the 'I believe' and a renunciation of the Devil:

'Holy Michael Archangel, defend us in the day of battle; be our safeguard against the wickedness and snares of the Devil. May God rebuke him, we humbly pray; and do thou Prince of the heavenly host, by the power of God thrust down to Hell Satan and all wicked spirits who wander through the world for the ruin of souls. Amen.' (Composed by Pope Leo XIII)

– Before Vatican II, this prayer used to be said after every Mass and most of the Faithful knew it by heart. Has the Devil taken advantage of its absence to make himself less visible, and hence much more dangerous as a result? Learn it and say it daily to make sure that he will not do so.

Most of us read the newspapers to keep abreast of what is going on in our country. We may also read books about our work or special interests. Television provides some serious programmes which catch our attention. How many of us, however, regularly read a Catholic/Christian newspaper or magazine? When did we last buy or read a religious book, a book about the one subject which reduces all others to insignificance, namely, our spiritual health and future? (Refer to page 159, first paragraph.)

Now, pause to consider your spiritual health.
Say a prayer and make a resolution.
Resolve to keep it !

Finally, what does St Benedict mean by *lectio divina* (sacred reading)? He rated it essential to holiness and we should too.

7

Why Did God Make Me?

This is the fundamental question. The answer given in the 'Penny' Catechism, *A Catechism of Christian Doctrine* (CCD, first published in 1889 and still commonly available) is clear and succinct: **'God made me to know Him, love Him and serve *(obey)* Him in this world, and to be happy with Him for ever in the next'** Also see Prologue I of the *Catechism of the Catholic Church* (Hereafter the acronym CCC). The truth is that man can only take his meaning from God, his loving Creator. What a tremendous value that gives each one of us?

To counter the increasing emphasis on the material advancement of the human race before all else, the meaning of the second part of the Catechism answer should be clearly seen as: '... **in order to** be happy with Him for ever in the next'. The happiness promised will not be in this world but in the next. In view of the suffering and unremitting deprivation of so many in this world, their wretchedness and misery, spiritual as well as physical, could it in all fairness be otherwise?

To achieve this happiness each one of us must save his or her soul, a very difficult and demanding task. It would be impossible without the help of the loving Creator Who made me, keeps me in being and has given me all I have – anything of which He can take away from me at any time.*

The greatest enemy is self, endlessly ingenious or quite ruthless in pursuit of its own ends, limitless in its power to persuade itself to do what it wants, especially in the sexual sphere.

---

* Were you reminded of this at the untimely death of Diana, Princess of Wales? Were you also aware that many other young mothers died suddenly and unexpectedly that night? And indeed die every night? Pray for all of them and their orphaned children.

7 WHY DID GOD MAKE ME?

The unhappy consequences of man's egoism are to be seen everywhere, especially in the poverty, slums, homelessness and deprivation of so many people. We can, and many do, offer some relief but only God can make a new world free from such destitution. He will do it at our request by changing hearts and minds. It is up to us and applies especially – and first – to our own attitude and conduct. What are we doing about this? **In particular, what am I doing about changing me?**

'I consecrate to Thee, my God, every beat of my heart, every breath and every movement of my body, every thought and every word; and with my whole being I desire to sing to Thee a long hymn of praise, of expiation of my sins, and of thanksgiving for Thy benefits.

'Speak, for Thy servant heareth, but help Thou my weakness.'

Cardinal Merry del Val, 1865–1930

The son of a Spanish marquis and an English mother, Rafael spent some time in Ushaw (seminary) but was ordained in Rome in 1888. Appointed at very short notice Secretary of the Conclave which elected Pope (Saint) Pius X, he served with distinction as his Cardinal Secretary of State throughout Pius's reign. Then appointed Archpriest of St Peter's, he lies buried in the Basilica. He was remarkable for his humility, sanctity and service to the poor, and the cause for his canonisation was introduced in 1953.

✠

In view of my complete dependence on God, is it not a vital and urgent priority to find out how to 'know Him, love Him and serve Him in this world' in order to save my soul 'and be happy with Him for ever in the next'? And to do everything possible to help my neighbour save his or her soul too? 'Love your neighbour as yourself' is the Second Commandment in the Gospels (Luke 10:27).

Second Commandment? Yes indeed; it is not the first, and it is not the first priority. Found in both the Old and the New Testaments, it can be our cue to return to the Bible.

Before doing so I should like to give four quotations from the daily religious column of *The Hindu*, a quality newspaper in English circulating throughout South India.

1. 'Devotion along with performance of duty has been prescribed by one of our greatest saints to enable man to steer through his life's voyage safely. Spelt out by Saint Madhwacharya, devotion incorporates love of God and acquisition of spiritual knowledge. Duty includes observance of the austerities named in the Scriptures and also doing service to humanity, as an indispensable part of it' (27: iii: 94).
2. 'Man is the architect of his own destiny and it is in his hands [to utilise his life] to realise God instead of frittering it away in the pursuit of material pleasures through discrimination. Mind is the source of all our aspirations and desires. Through proper control and training it is important to utilise it to pursue eternal values ... Man must take recourse to the Scriptures to adopt the path of right action' (29: iii: 95).
3. 'In spite of extraordinary care the devotee may easily be led astray from the path by the mire of delusion. The senses are so powerful as to draw the mind away from the chosen divine ideal. Hence he should constantly engage himself in spiritual practices to discipline his mind and harbour only sublime thoughts. As the mind prompted by the sense organs can run after pleasures, it will engage itself in all kinds of activities except the one that leads him to Godhood' (20: iii: 93).
4. 'The Jeevar Swami of Ahobila Math said all people can adopt the procedure of "surrender" and God would grant them

salvation. To be eligible one should do everything according to God's will, abstain from acts which would incur His displeasure, display total faith in His dispensation and always feel humble. Some ask whether anyone has seen Moksha [domain of the Lord] and demand proof. Can these men categorically assert that there is no such kingdom? What is the evidence for their negation? In the absence of anything contrary, we should believe in its existence. All contribute to this view. Even otherwise, clinging to God's feet will be akin to getting vaccinated. Total submission to God would make the Almighty respond to our entreaties' (6: iii: 95).

Having clipped these quotations at the time because, with only a few minor context changes, they struck me as being so very true, I felt that they had to be included in this book as an example of how much Hinduism and Christianity have in common. Do the passages not show glimpses of 'absolute Truth, which, like beauty itself, floats elusive, obscure, half submerged, in the silent still waters of mystery'? *Lord Jim*, Joseph Conrad (1857–1924).

However, there is no salvation outside the one, Holy, Catholic and Apostolic Church, although followers of other religions, or none, can be saved under certain conditions

Our loving God is both just and merciful.

'Lord, teach me to see through "what everyone is doing" and turn me away from "I will do it too". Not my will but Thine be done!' (See Chapters 14 and 41.)

✠

And finally, a searching question: 'Am I a self-addict? How much is self-interest a moral basis of my conduct?'

8
Is Jesus the Son of God?

Back to the Bible we turn to the New Testament, in particular the four Gospels, the story of Jesus Christ who, like his foster father, was a carpenter. Jesus claimed to be the Son of God; is it true?

First, the sheer number of believers, Christians past and present, and especially the lives of a countless host of saints and martyrs, is strong encouragement – at the very least – that it is true. Second, the extraordinary story of the man Jesus Christ, His Mother being the Virgin Mary, is unlikely to have been made up. (The name Jesus means 'saviour' (Hebrew), and Christ 'anointed' (Greek).) Certainly there has been nothing like it since. Third, His life, and especially the miracles He wrought, fulfilled prophecies in the Old Testament. (Note the significance of this: here is a proven link between the Old Testament and the New, despite their having been written so many centuries apart.) Finally, after horrendous suffering and death by crucifixion, Jesus rose from His tomb on the third day and forty days later ascended into Heaven.

This extraordinary story is told independently in their Gospels by four very different men, Matthew, Mark, Luke and John, three apostles and an associate of Paul. Remarkable! After hearing the story, or reading any of the four Gospels, who could fail to believe that an exceptional man, Jesus Christ, lived on earth two thousand years ago? In fact, He was an ordinary young man, growing up like any other boy to the age of thirty. Then it was His claim to be the Son of God, and the miracles He wrought, and how He came to be acknowledged by the people, which set Him apart from His fellows and made Him exceptional. His death on the Cross and His rising from the tomb conclusively proclaimed His true identity.

8 IS JESUS THE SON OF GOD?

We can believe with certainty that Jesus is the Son of God, the Second Person of the Holy Trinity. It is the central mystery on which the Faith of all Christians rests.

To remind ourselves of His suffering and death in order to bring salvation to all sinners and restore the supernatural life of our souls, let us recall and meditate upon the Stations of the Cross.

Since few of us can quote all fourteen, especially in their order, here they are:

Stations of the Cross:

I	Jesus is condemned to death
II	Jesus receives the cross
III	Jesus falls the first time under His cross
IV	Jesus is met by His Blessed Mother
V	The cross is laid upon Simon of Cyrene
VI	Veronica wipes the face of Jesus
VII	Jesus falls the second time
VIII	The women of Jerusalem mourn for our Lord
IX	Jesus falls for the third time
X	Jesus is stripped of His garments
XI	Jesus is nailed to the cross
XII	Jesus dies on the cross
XIII	Jesus is taken down from the cross
XIV	Jesus is placed in the sepulchre

– Imagine, if you can, the pain of flesh torn by brutal lashing, of a skull pierced by sharp thorns, of bones bruised and chafing, of hands and feet pierced by driven nails, of a battered body, covered with buzzing flies, hanging in the greatest discomfort on a cross; such agony endured unto death for the redemption of mankind from sin is dreadful to contemplate. All of this was for me ...
– After so much suffering by His Son to redeem us sinners, what pain must God feel when we reject His love, as so many in the world have done? Can you hear Jesus crying: 'My God, My God, why are My children forsaking Me?'

9

His Church

Jesus died to redeem mankind. He rose again on the third day. The Gospels tell us this. Continuing, they tell us Jesus Christ also founded His Church, that which the Catholic Church maintains She is, and admission into which is by Baptism. In particular, He guaranteed that 'the powers of death [in Greek: the gates of Hell] shall not prevail against it' (Matthew 16:18), and He appointed guardians for the Faithful.

(What is 'Hell'? The word derives from the Hebrew *Sheol* meaning the underworld, the abode of the dead or departed spirits, according to the Shorter Oxford English Dictionary. Here is an example of how easy it can be when one wants to find the meaning of a word and starts looking. Were you successful in translating the French verse at the end of Chapter 4?)

The Faithful were to be led and guarded by His Apostle Peter, the first Pope, to whom He gave the Keys of the Kingdom (Matthew 16:19). He also changed his name from Simon. This is now the practice of his successors on election to the Papacy. Jesus chose him in spite of knowing that he would shortly deny Him thrice. Peter was a simple fisherman, quite ordinary, like most of us, but look what he achieved because he gave his life to Jesus!

Is this not a sign that it is because of our unworthiness that God seeks our devotion to Him? His love for us is merciful as well as constant.

Thenceforward the teaching of the Church would be unerring and binding, through an unbroken papal succession, until the end of time. How could it be otherwise? Left to himself, man only believes what suits him.

9 HIS CHURCH

Peter suffered martyrdom for his Faith. So, too, have nearly thirty other Popes, including St John I as late as AD 526.

The mission of God's Church is to glorify Him and achieve the salvation of our souls by their sanctification. It is not to devote all its efforts to try to achieve a better future for mankind on earth. The Church's mission is concerned with bettering our human condition, with justice that will provide the right conditions for Faith and love of God, and much is said about this in Catholic social teaching, but it would be a mistake to take that desire for justice out of the context of Faith, which humanism does. 'My Kingdom is not of this world', said the Lord. (John 18:36). Mary the Mother of God stressed at Fatima (1917) that the healing of the immortal soul was far more important than the healing of the mortal body.

It is those who do not believe in God who exclude from consideration any world but this and, therefore, seek all they desire here. This is secularism, a popular and growing trend.

The purpose for which God founded His Church is the sanctification of man, body as well as soul, for eternal life in His Kingdom.

'Salve Regina'

'Hail, holy Queen, Mother of Mercy; hail our life, our sweetness, and our hope! To thee do we cry, poor banished children of Eve: to thee do we send up our sighs, mourning and weeping in this vale of tears. Turn, then, most gracious advocate, thine eyes of mercy towards us; and after this our exile, show unto us the blessed fruit of thy womb, Jesus.

O clement, O loving, O sweet Virgin Mary.

℣ Pray for us, O holy Mother of God
℟ That we may be made worthy of the promises of Christ

'Let ue pray: O God our refuge and our strength, look down in mercy on Thy people who cry to Thee; and by the intercession of the glorious and Immaculate Virgin Mary, Mother of God, of Saint Joseph her spouse, of Thy blessed Apostles Peter and Paul, and of all the saints, in mercy and goodness hear our prayers for the conversion of sinners, and for the liberty and exaltation of our holy mother the Church. Through the same Christ our Lord. Amen.'

– In 1884, Pope Leo XIII ordered that after Low Mass there should be recited three *Ave Marias**, *the Salve Regina* followed by a prayer to Our Lady, and the prayer to Saint Michael (see page 24 or 61). A ten-year indulgence could be earned.

– Pius X in 1904 recommended the addition of a three-fold invocation to the Sacred Heart of Jesus:

'Most Sacred Heart of Jesus, have mercy on us' (three times). It carried an indulgence of seven years and seven quarantines ('About Indulgences': CCC 1471–9).

– The reciting of these prayers with the Faithful was discontinued after Vatican II.

– Take note of the punctuation of the prayers in this book and, indeed, of all prayers you may read: it is designed to slow the saying of them with pauses and so enable the meaning of each phrase to be savoured.

✠

Christians reading this who are not Catholics accepting the infallible authority on Faith and morals of the Pope in Rome, Christ's Vicar on earth, should remember that until the Reformation, the Church, Christian and Catholic, Holy and Apostolic, was one, a united assembly of the Faithful. The breakaway, partly a lay and partly a religious rebellion against the obedience to Her teaching demanded by the Church, occurred after fifteen hundred years of

---

* The Three Hail Marys prayed twice daily, urged St Alphonsus de Liguori, are the best safeguard to chastity. Look around you: are they not again so much needed?

9 HIS CHURCH

astonishing growth and dynamism. It is only in the last four hundred years that branches from the trunk, still standing tall and straight like a cedar of Lebanon, have sought independence and autonomy from Rome.

Today we see men and women breaking away as individuals and setting their own rules as they pursue their own ends. The culture and politics of the world have no time for religion, the acknowledgement of absolute Truth, of intrinsic right and wrong, and anthropocentric man has become his own god, responsible only to himself. Will he be called to account at his death?

Death is an event man can neither predict nor avoid. No one has returned to speak of the hereafter – except one man, Jesus Christ. What has He told us? He gave us an instruction: 'Follow Me.' Is that the answer you expected? How would an atheist or an agnostic react? How would you explain it?

But to return to the Church. 'The universal Church cannot err, since She is governed by the Holy Ghost, Who is the Spirit of truth: for such was Our Lord's promise to His disciples (John 16:13): 'When He, the Spirit of truth is come, He will teach you all truth' (St Thomas Aquinas, 1226–74). While the exercise of the power of infallibility requires the assent of the Pope, all the teachings of the Church are nonetheless authoritative and must be obeyed.

Finally, do you know what are the six sins against the Holy Spirit? Let me give them: presumption, despair, resisting the known truth, envy of another's spiritual good, obstinacy in sin and final impenitence. The odd numbers – one, three and five – are those that I need especially to keep in mind when I pray 'Lead me not into temptation'; I am confident, however, that 'Holy Mary, Mother of God' can protect me, and you too, from the sixth, 'now, and at the hour of my death'.

[**A test**: why is harmony between *lex orandi* (law of worship) and *lex credendi* (law of faith) so essential to the Church?]

10

Our Mortality

Before examining in more detail what Christ's Church teaches, here is a guiding general precept: it is prudent to incline towards acceptance of authoritative teaching rather than disagreement with it. To this can be added: try to establish the context and thus the reason behind any particular teaching which may be troubling or feel uncomfortable.

The Church does not need to teach that we are mortal. We all know because we see mortality around us. We know we are going to die sometime, but generally we are not unhappy people and are grateful for life whatever our state. Especially, however, we should be thankful that we are unlikely to be called to an early test of Faith as searching as martyrdom. This should be an incentive to pray to God through the host of saints who did give up their lives, often in agony after unspeakable torment, rather than deny their loving Saviour, Jesus Christ, and His teaching. 'He who loses his life for My sake will find it' (Matthew 10:39). There are no greater heroes and heroines than the martyrs who refused to put this world's demands or fashionable behaviour before those of God, their Creator, and the thousands who died to safeguard the Mass.

While we may not be called upon to die for our Faith like the martyrs, we are called upon to live for it. Be assured, however, that if we were called to the final witness of martyrdom, we should be given the grace to accept and endure it, for God never asks the impossible of us.

We are indeed called upon to live for our Faith and the testing time for us may well be short, shorter than expected. Who can be sure to be alive ten years hence, or next month, or even twenty-four hours from now? ('For tomorrow and its needs I do not pray. Keep me, Lord, just for today.') The only certainty is death – but not the time it will strike – and death will be followed by a judgment, an inspection, when we hand back the life we have had on loan.

The death of many may well coincide with the consummation of the world which can also reliably be expected, perhaps sooner rather than later. Whatever has a beginning must have an end.

Pope John Paul II has told us that the ending of a year, especially, should make Christians think about the end of time and God's plan for eternal salvation. He has also reminded us that the world is under the power of evil and that the Antichrist will come before the end of the world (see Matthew 24:3–44).

While most people, fortunately, are spared the fear of unexpected catastrophe and sudden or early death, we must keep in mind our weakness and the certainty of our mortality, that from the moment of our birth we have been dying; we are all on our way to our deaths. Then we shall meet the God Who made us, keeps us and loves us.

Be not afraid of death:

'I want to see God and, in order to see Him, I must die.'

St Teresa of Avila

'I am not dying: I am entering life.' St Thérèse of Lisieux

Have we strayed from the teaching of His Church as to why we were created? Do we love God as a person? Are we doing His will? Are we looking forward to our death? Are we prepared for death whenever it may come?

'I confess to Almighty God, to blessed Mary ever Virgin, to blessed Michael the Archangel, to blessed John the Baptist, to the holy Apostles Peter and Paul, our holy father St Benedict and

all the saints, that I have sinned exceedingly, through my fault, through my fault, through my most grievous fault.' (I am using the version taught to me by the Benedictine monks at Ampleforth. The name of your patron saint or any other can be substituted for Benedict, the father of monasticism in Europe.)

Here we pause and examine our conscience for commissions and omissions displeasing to our loving God.

'Therefore I beseech the Blessed Mary ever Virgin, blessed Michael the Archangel, blessed John the Baptist, the holy Apostles Peter and Paul, our holy father St Benedict and all the saints, to pray for me to the Lord our God. Amen.'

It should be followed by an Act of Contrition, and one can be found in Chapter 24 on page 80.

Meanwhile, a sincere 'My God, I am sorry' is enough, if it is accompanied by a firm resolve not to offend again.

– It may be considered early to introduce this discipline before we have dealt with the subject of conscience (Chapter 41), but is it not prudent always to be prepared? Remember the story of the foolish virgins (Matthew 25:1–13).

– Remember, too, that no one is immune from temptation at any time of the day or night.

'Jesus, should my love for Thee prove weak when I am tempted to turn away from Thee in sin, may I so fear Hell that it will stand as an ultimate deterrent.'

✠

Did you know that in the Church's Calendar of Saints(1962), one hundred feast days are devoted to those titled Confessor, only seventy-six fewer than for Her Martyrs?

When did you last go to Confession? (See page 55 para. 2.)

Remeber these source acronyms used throughtout the book
CCC:*Catechism of the Catholic Church; Fidei Depositum*, 1994
CCD:*A Catechism of Christian Doctrine; the 'Penny' Catechism.*

Bad Popes

'What about the bad Popes?' is the question used to cast doubt on the infallible (unerring) teaching of the Church, and to open the way to championing conscience over Her teaching in matters of moral conduct. There have indeed been a number of bad Popes and this is very sad. Even Peter denied our Lord thrice (Mark 14:66–72). All men, however, suffer from Original Sin, are weak, worldly people, and Satan is tireless in his battling to capture their souls. Popes, being leaders of high profile, are especially attractive targets, no less in need of grace and, therefore, vulnerable too. Remember, however, that Jesus promised that the gates of Hell would not prevail against His Church.

In spite of bad Popes, no instruction binding on the Faithful contrary to Faith or morals has ever been promulgated. Moreover the doctrinal teaching of the Church, like any truth, has been unchanging and consistent. Until the Reformation in the sixteenth century, this was acknowledged by all Christians. At that time there was a split-off from the Church and only the Roman Catholic Faithful continued to accept the supremacy and infallibility of the Supreme Pontiff in Rome.

This means that while a Pope may stray, the Church he leads – and this is Christ's promise – will certainly not. There should be rejoicing and gratitude that there have been so many saints in the Holy See in the unbroken line of succession from Peter, heads chosen by the Holy Spirit of a Church which has been one, Holy, Catholic and Apostolic for over two thousand years. It is an establishment unique in all human history. No other has existed for so long nor been so consistent.

Are you aware that it is not the rich and famous of this world who punctuate the pages of history and are most remembered? It is those who worked only for the Church and for God. Moreover, it is Christian churches which are the most common landmarks for so many people as well as their chosen venues for Christening, marriage and funeral rites.

As stated above, the Church will not stray from the Truth; this is Christ's promise. Since all human minds are capable of error, had only a deposit of truth been left for our own interpretation, we should soon have destroyed its certainty. **Therefore, to preserve the Truth, God made His Church infallible.** The whole Truth has not been revealed but we are progressively seeing more of it, probing it and gaining greater insight. What Truth has been revealed has been infallibly so, that is, without error, in any definition of Faith or morals.

Denial of this rock of certainty puts members of the Church at sixes and sevens and results in evident disintegration. 'And if a house is divided against itself, that house will not be able to stand' (Mark 3:25). Without a guarantee, the truth is whatever anyone says it is: His Word is lost. Lives are lived independent of God, who is Truth, and the only accountability is to oneself. Look around and see how our society is suffering in the disorder of conflicting egoist lifestyles; in particular, take note of the spread of individual lawless behaviour and, in its pursuit against it, the consequent infringement of social and human rights by civil authority. Thus, there is decreasing harmony between authorities and the people they should be serving, a trend bound to intensify. The once high standing of our political leaders, all of whom are now career politicians, most of undistinguished qualifying experience, has fallen dramatically. Respect for authority is much diminished. Sadly this even applies to the authority of the Church.

11 BAD POPES

Prayer to St Peter:

'Thou art the Shepherd of the sheep, O Prince of the Apostles: to thee were given the keys of the Kingdom of Heaven.

℣ Thou art Peter

℞ And upon this Rock I shall build My Church.

Let us pray.

'Raise us up we beseech Thee, O Lord, by the apostolic might of Thy blessed Apostle, Peter, that the weaker we are in ourselves the more powerful may be the assistance whereby we are strengthened through his intercession; that thus, ever fortified by the protection of Thine Apostle, we may never yield to sin nor be overwhelmed by adversity. Through Christ Our Lord. Amen.'

✠

Note: Galileo is used as a stick with which to attack the infallibility of the Pope, although his transgression was not a matter of Faith or morals but disobedience. In fact no papal condemnation of Galileo was issued. There is much more to his case than is generally known and it is a story worth studying. Start with pages 207–12 of *Creation Rediscovered* by G. J. Keane, which is in the Book List.

To close this chapter, I should like to quote a poem predicting a Slavonic Pope which was written in 1850 by the Polish poet Julius Stowacki:

'In an age of discord

God rings the massive bell, a clarion call:

There is an empty throne for a Slavonic Pope,

The sun radiating from his face is a beacon for his followers,

Ever-growing throngs and tribes will follow him

Towards the Light where is God.
Listening to his prayers and his commands
Not only will the people hear him but the sun will stop.
Because there is power
Because there is a miracle
And power is indeed needed to raise up this world to God.
So here he comes, this Slavonic Pope – brother of the peoples of all nations.
He will distribute love as generously as, today, the leaders of the world
Distribute their guns.
His spiritual power will take the whole world in his hands.
He will bring new health, he will bring light and love
And save the world.
He will sweep out the interiors of the Churches,
Even their very porches.
He will show the place of God in the creation of the world
As clearly as the light of day.'

This was uttered over a hundred years ago and is in the tradition of the Old Testament prophecies. Truly remarkable! Look again at the detail: did you know that there is an authenticated case of the sun having stopped in Egypt, an event which took place several times and was seen by huge numbers of ordinary people? Read, also, the story of Fatima (refer to Book List*).

Finally, here is some general advice on prayer from C.S. Lewis which is most helpful:

'Speak less about God and more to Him'.

C.S. Lewis, 1898-1963, an English scholar and writer, was the author of the well-known *Screwtape Letters*(see Book List).

---

* The Book List now has some useful web resources. (Page 164)

12

Judgment at Death

Let us go back to that important word 'judgment' mentioned in Chapter 10. Surely a loving, merciful God would not condemn those whom He created? But it is not He who condemns anyone. We behave badly; we choose to break His law; we put our own wishes before His will; we twist His words; thereby it is we who rebuff Him and, rejecting His love, condemn ourselves. **'I tell you, on the day of judgment men will render account of every careless word they utter; for by your words you will be justified and by your words you will be condemned' (Matthew 12:37).** In justice, there must be a judge; God is Justice and He is the perfect Judge.

Second, consider Hitler or Stalin, singling out as examples two documented bloodstained tyrants. Focus next on Mother Teresa, humble, prayerful, saving souls and relieving distress. Does not common sense and natural justice suggest that the former should suffer for their evil deeds against mankind and its Creator, and that the latter should enjoy the favour of Him she has served so selflessly? The laws of men mete out punishment to the guilty in this life, so why not a judgment under God's law at death to separate the sheep from the goats before entry into His Eternal Kingdom (see Matthew 25:31–46)?

We must accept, however, that the Judgment of God is totally beyond the minds of men and women, as indeed is the suffering on this earth of the innocent. This is not a reason angrily to reject God. It should draw us closer to Him, so that we long to look on the face of the One Whose love seems so far beyond us and yet is so strong for each one of us.

Read the Book of Job in the Old Testament, a story of great calamities. It is not an easy read. With the aid of a commentary, winkle out the encouragement there is in this tale of dreadful suffering.

'O God, keep me on the path of achieving happiness and success that are real.
'Keep my vision always clear to see the goals.
'Help me to tap the hidden powers within and above me.
'Give me the strength to work with all the energies of my mind and body.
'Help me to practise the love of people and service to others.
'Keep me for ever with a smile on my face for the whole human race.'

H. J. Kaiser 1882–1967

Kaiser was an outstanding American industrialist. His interests were dams, bridges, cement, aluminium and automobiles. In particular, he applied his skills to shipbuilding during World War II, especially Liberty ships: he was able to build a 10,500-ton freighter in less than five days and was responsible for one third of the US merchant shipping built during the war. He was also a philanthropist, so typical of outstandingly successful American businessmen.

Like each person whom He creates God gave him unique gifts, some small, some great; at our Judgment He will ask what gifts we bring Him in return.

A Divine Promise:
When He appeared to St Margaret Mary Alacoque, our

12 JUDGMENT AT DEATH

Lord promised to those who receive the Holy Eucharist on the first Friday of nine consecutive months the grace of final penitence. 'They shall not die in my disgrace,' He told her, 'nor without receiving their sacraments: My divine Heart shall be their safe refuge in their last moment.'

St Margaret Mary Alacoque, virgin, 1647–90: born in France, she entered a Visitation convent in 1671 and became our Lord's instrument of His revelation with regard to His Sacred Heart and the meaning and purpose of the Blessed Sacrament. Look her up in Butler's *Lives of the Saints*. Take advantage of His promise at the next first Friday

To conclude this chapter on Judgment at Death, let us focus on Jesus the Son of God, hanging nailed to the Cross, broken and bleeding, in unimaginable agony, suffering for us, you and me whom He loves so much, as He yields His life to redeem us from all our sins. Just before He bowed His head and gave up His spirit, He cried out 'It is finished', sometimes translated, 'It is accomplished.' (John 19:30.) May we, when we come to die, be able to say like Him, 'I have completed the task given to me; I have chosen to do Thy Will.' (See Cardinal Newman page 26)

I referred briefly to the Antichrist in the previous chapter (page 41): how often have you given any thought to this figure? Here is a quotation to ponder. Fr Martin D'Arcy, a Farm Street Jesuit of great renown who in his later years spent much of his time in America, warned of the Antichrist, 'the libidinous ape, the great deceiver who calls lust love, avarice fulfilment, peace the loosening of all ties of loyalty, and who invites surrender to immediate gratification'. That was in Los Angeles in 1971; what would he be saying today?

One further thought: we have been told that the Antichrist will present himself as a messenger of peace and security; are these not the very objectives being pursued by the secular humanist?

13

Eternity

We are taught by the Church that at the Last Judgment, when Christ returns in glory, it will be revealed 'that God's justice triumphs over all the injustices committed by His creatures and that God's love is stronger than death' (CCC 1040). Those in mortal sin (Chapter 24) will fall away from God into Hell; others who are repentant will be committed to cleansing in Purgatory; and there is reward in Heaven for the souls who have accepted His loving salvation by doing only His Will.

Certainly there will be a judgment, and belief in Heaven and Hell is an article of Catholic Faith (Chapter 21). Into Hell will go those sinners who have refused to give God their obedience and their love, not only in their outward words and actions but also in their innermost thoughts and desires. To Purgatory, but only for an interim, go those whose penance and suffering on earth have not been sufficient reparation for their sins. For the cleansed, and all the men and women who have not failed to return His love by doing His Will, the reward will be Eternal Life with Him in Heaven. Exactly what these three states are, however, is a mystery and will remain so until we die.

The nature of Eternal Life is one of many mysteries of our Faith, and there should be no surprise at the existence of any of them. Are there not mysteries aplenty all around us which are easily accepted? While some may well be explained as our knowledge grows, there are those which even the greatest human intellects admit are unlikely ever to be solved in this life. Amen – so be it.

Amen, too, with regard to the mysteries of the Catholic Faith. Many can be explored through study to increase our understanding

13 ETERNITY

and trust – 'enlivening our Faith' – but all will remain until the end of time. Surely it is better to have something personal, something promising, however mysterious, to which to look forward after this world – 'to be happy with Him for ever in the next' – than nothing at all? (What is there to lose?) Even the most primitive peoples believe in a hereafter for the spirits of their dead and have strict rules of conduct to be followed in order to achieve their hallowed Nirvana or destiny.

We shall all die. We shall also be dead for a long, long time. I recall that someone described 'being' as a deeply mysterious and delightful and astounding thing. Can we imagine 'not being', now or after death?

What did St Paul say about our life after death? 'Run that you may obtain the prize.'

An athlete intent on Olympic gold, indeed anyone keen to achieve a desired physical objective, will work at it. Exercises, training, study of technique, the advice of a coach, vigorous practice, rigorous diet, continence by a married man or woman, early nights and mornings: all these will feature in the quest to excel and win. The privation, even pain, suffered in this self-discipline is soon forgotten; the satisfaction of achievement remembered through old age and to death.

Compared to eternity, life is only an instant; the body is mortal but the soul immortal. Do we work to achieve our immortal goal, a prize against which a gold medal is but a speck?

Listen to St Paul: 'Every athlete exercises self-control in all things. They do it to receive a perishable wreath, but we an imperishable. Well, I do not run aimlessly ...' (1 Corinthians 9:25–6).

Ask yourself: do I run aimlessly?

'Homesick for Heaven, we ask for Thy help, dear Mother and Queen of Heaven. Look on the sorrows and sadness of so many people, on the blindness to life hereafter of so many more, and speak for us all to Thy Son. Like a kind mother, lead us to Him.'

14

'Thy Will be Done'

Trust comes easily to innocent minds. Did not our Lord say: 'Unless you be like little children ...' (Matthew 18:1–4)? They have innocent minds and understand in simple terms. **There is nothing complex, however, about the Will of God if we put our minds to it instead of to our own will.** Children trust their parents; God is our loving Father and we should trust Him. Surely He will provide us with everything we need to gain the eternal reward He promises us and wants us to have? As already stated in Chapter 10, He does not command the impossible.

To qualify for something happy to which to look forward, it is necessary, remembering the First Commandment, to worship the one true God, our Loving Creator, and, therefore, 'to serve Him', to do His Will. Indeed 'Thy will be done' is part of the Lord's Prayer taught by Jesus Christ, as it is recorded in the Gospel (Matthew 6:9–13). Using simple language, it is the second prayer we commonly learn as children. The first is the 'Hail Mary' (*Ave Maria*). 'Full of grace', Mary accepted to do the Will of God: 'Be it done to me according to Thy Word', which she was able to declare because she was full of grace (Luke 1:38).

No need here to imagine pictures in our minds; there are many wonderful paintings of the Virgin Mary with which we are all familiar and can recall. But for how much longer, I wonder, will they appear on Christmas cards to remind everyone of the birth of Christ? A great Christian feast has become just a commercial break, a time to spend, spend, spend, almost an orgy of self-indulgence and yielding to Mammon.

What if Mary had decided – as she was perfectly free to do – not to accept the Will of God? Think about this for a few minutes. Then rejoice at her *'Fiat'* (Luke 1:38) and her *'Magnificat'* (Luke 1: 46–55): thereby her son, Jesus Christ, the Son of God, was able to redeem mankind and found His Church for our salvation. What a huge debt we owe to her! And to her husband Joseph for his loving support.

The *'Ave Maria'*:
'Hail Mary, full of grace, the Lord is with thee; blessed art thou among women, and blessed is the fruit of thy womb Jesus. Holy Mary, Mother of God, pray for us sinners, now, and at the hour of our death. Amen.'
– The more we think about this prayer, the more meaning the words have. Occasionally it may be better to say it once very, very slowly than to say a decade of the Rosary. Meditation and contemplation are so important to the sanctification of our souls, yet in our noisy, busy lives few of us find the time and quiet moments needed; but we must keep trying – every day. There is certainly no excuse for the inattention of most of us to the meaning of the words of familiar prayers.

Do you remember what Jesus said to Philip at the Last Supper? 'If you love Me, you will keep My commandments. He who loves My commandments and keeps them, he it is who loves Me' (John 14:15 and 21). We cannot love God and then, to suit ourselves, decide by our own natural power what is good and what is evil, what we should or should not do. That is a return to Original Sin (see Chapter 3).

15

Why a Church?

As a result of man's disobedience and fall, no one can begin to know God's Will and then do it without the necessary grace. Original Sin is forgiven and the first grace is bestowed on us at Baptism. Even Jesus Christ, the son of God Who had become man, was baptised – in the river Jordan by John the Baptist (Matthew 3:13–17).

In the traditional Mass, the priest and the congregation genuflect at the words in the *Credo* which record the greatest event in the history of mankind, *'Et incarnatus est'* which translate 'And He was made man'. In the *Novus Ordo Missae* all should make a reverent bow here. It is rarely practised, a small failing among many more serious lapses following the Church's easing of a traditional instruction (see 'Fasting' in Chapter 25).

Since all that the Church teaches is in the Gospels, which, as we have noted, link to the Old Testament of the Bible, why is it necessary to have a church, to be a member of it and to accept its teaching? Why can people not do what they feel is right, guided by the Bible? Alternatively, can people not just be Christians, followers of Christ, and do what He taught as recorded in the Gospels? They would be leading Christian lives, loving and mindful of their neighbour, and kept from doing evil by their consciences.

Two of the reasons will be given here.

One: Jesus Christ founded His Church for us, the men and women He has created (Matthew 16:18). He has given us the Sacraments, including Holy Communion, the Sacrament of the Eucharist, the food of His Body consecrated in Holy Mass by His ordained priest. He has also given us the Sacrament of Penance and Reconciliation, whereby the sins we commit and wholeheartedly repent of can be forgiven in confession. 'And when [Jesus] had said this, He breathed on [the disciples] and said to them: "Receive the Holy Spirit. If you forgive the sins of any, they are forgiven; if you retain the sins of any, they are retained." ' (John 20:23; also Matthew 16:19.)

The Sacraments of Penance and Reconciliation and the Eucharist are miracles. Jesus offers them to us through His ordained priests, Sacraments bearing His grace which we can receive frequently. How can we ignore miracles which promise so much? Do we, indeed, realise that they are miracles? In particular, the immense and immediate consolation of being able to speak to God's ordained priest, living and accessible, for the forgiveness of our sin, and to seek advice as well as saving grace, is surely something to marvel at. We are allowing God to show us His mercy and understanding. To go on to possess Him after Holy Communion is a privilege without equal.

To receive the Body of Christ in the Blessed Sacrament unworthily is a sacrilege and a mortal sin. The fasting from midnight required before Vatican II was a penance, a small discipline of self, a reminder that it was necessary to be in a state of grace. If not, or if in doubt about the stain of a mortal sin, then advice and absolution had to be sought in Confession. The fasting has been shortened to one hour; has this reduced the guilt and shame many sinners should feel? For while the number of communicants increases, the number going to Confession has seriously declined. Be warned by St Paul (1 Corinthians 11:27–9) and do not risk profanity for want of more frequent Confession.

The Church, therefore, exists to teach everyone 'the way, the truth and the life' (John 14: 6), to sanctify our bodies as well as our souls, to help us thoroughly to inform our conscience (see Chapter 41) and to be the channel through which we receive God's grace. Without grace our souls are lost.

Two: a second reason why we need to be practising members of His Church is this: Satan is roaming the world – he is not alone; he has a host of henchmen – to take advantage of our fallen nature, to persuade people that they should please only themselves, be comfortable, gratify themselves, exploit their neighbours, grab power; in short to do what they want and make the most of life. Self-gratification is the lure for the Devil's conquests and they reject God. The presence of Satan must never be overlooked, and his power and that of his demons, the other fallen angels, should never be underestimated. Did not the Devil even put Jesus to temptation no less than three times, as is recorded in the Gospels (Matthew 4:1–11)? We must stand fast against him, united together to beat him off.

The Church is Christ living in the world. We believe Him. He is infallible. We are safe in His Mystical Body – provided we do His Will. It is the Church that teaches us His Will 'in the name of the Father, the Son and the Holy Spirit'. It is from the Holy Spirit that the Church receives its authority and unerring guidance; our obedience is our salvation.

'Grant us we beseech Thee, O Lord, fervently to desire, wisely to search out, and perfectly to fulfil all that is well pleasing unto Thee. May our path to Thee, we pray, be safe, straightforward, and perfect to the end. Give us, O Lord, a steadfast heart, which no unworthy affection may drag down. Give us an unconquered heart, which no tribulation can wear out: give us an upright heart, which no unworthy purpose may tempt aside. Give me understanding to know Thee, and a faithfulness that may finally embrace Thee. Through Jesus Christ Our Lord.'

St Thomas Aquinas (1226–74)

15 WHY A CHURCH?

Theologian and doctor of the Church, one of the great guardians of the Church, St Thomas can be found in Butler's *Lives of the Saints*, which is in the Book List.

– Also, look up the lives of St Augustine and the two saints who were quoted in Chapter 10.

✠

The liturgy of the Church has much to teach us. We should benefit immensely from more frequent acquaintance with it than just at Sunday Mass. Study a Roman Missal during Lent, time of preparation and penance before those awesome events, the Passion, Crucifixion and Resurrection of Christ, which are the promise of salvation, provided only that we seek His sanctifying grace.

The Russian rite in Lent constantly repeats the prayer of St Ephraem the Syrian. We could memorise it and say it regularly:

'O Lord and Master of my life!
Take from me the spirit of sloth,
faint-heartedness, lust for power and idle talk,
But give rather the spirit of chastity,
humility, patience and love to Thy servant.
Yea, O Lord, and King!
Grant me to see my own errors
and not to judge my brother;
For Thou art blessed unto ages of ages. Amen.'

Ephraem (306–73), convert, deacon, confessor and Doctor of the Church, lived as a hermit most of his life. A great champion of the Faith, he was renowned for his explanations of the Scriptures and as a writer of hymns in honour of Our Lady and the Saints.

✠

16

My Guardian Angel

This is a suitable place to remind ourselves that each of us has been given a guardian angel to guide us and keep us on track (CCC 336). God does indeed love us and, even knowing that we shall defy Him, never ceases to be merciful to us when we turn back to Him. He wants us to choose Him, to stay with Him. We can be hugely encouraged, too, by the experience of the good thief: by just proclaiming his belief, he was given a promise by Jesus: '"This day you will be with Me in Paradise"' (Luke 23:39–43). (A definition of Paradise on which to meditate: 'not elsewhere without Me'.)

What is an angel? What does one look like? How many are there? Are there different kinds? What do they all do? Mentioned in both the Old and New Testaments, they first appeared in Genesis: Lucifer, the greatest of them, but who defied God, fell from grace and was seen in disguise as a serpent, surely a grim warning to us all. Later in the same book, two angels came to Sodom: they saved Lot and his two daughters but his wife, disobeying the Lord, turned into a pillar of salt (Genesis 19:1–26). Perhaps the best known is the Archangel Gabriel, but there were also Raphael and Michael. There are countless more.

Angels are ideal subjects for mental pictures. It is important to keep them in mind for 'the whole life of the Church benefits from the mysterious and powerful help of angels' (CCC 334). See what else you can find out about them.

'O Angel of God, whom God hath appointed to be my guardian, enlighten and protect, direct and guide me.

16 MY GUARDIAN ANGEL

'O Angel of God, remind me every day that only in Him do I live and move and have my being and that my heart shall not rest until it rests in Him.

'O Angel of God, be always at my side and lead me to Him.'

– Let us try never to forget the existence of our very own spiritual watchman. We could also remember the others, St Michael in particular, to our immense advantage.

– Picture an angel guarding just you, and always keep that picture in mind.

– There is another prayer which we were taught as children. It deserves to be recalled here for our children and grandchildren:

'Angel of God, my Guardian dear,
To whom His love commits me here,
Ever this day (night) be at my side,
To light and guard, to rule and guide.'

It should hang over every child's bed.

Others in Paradise who should not be forgotten are our patron saints. At Baptism we are given the name of a saint and at confirmation we choose another. They can be powerful allies, close to God, who are only too pleased to help us if we just ask them.

'St John the Evangelist, please ask God to bless all those who read this book, and may they each derive some small lasting benefit from it.'

✠

I regret not having had the space to put in the Litany of the Saints, the Church's most solemn call for help. Ask your parish priest for a copy and say it on the first day of every month. There is no more powerful a prayer, except for the *Te Deum*, that great hymn of thanksgiving to God always sung by the Church to celebrate His favour on a special occasion.

17

Satan

The Devil, otherwise Satan, is out of fashion. No longer commonly referred to, he has been pushed into dark recesses – or, more likely, has hidden himself from us – from which satanic rites surface from time to time in the reports of social workers and headlines in the press, only to disappear just as mysteriously. This poses no threat to most of us and little notice is taken. Another media event.

Yet Satan is extremely powerful and resourceful; we need help if we are to defeat him. His most successful ploy is to isolate an individual and appeal to their fallen nature on a single issue. Pride brought about his own downfall; he then engineered the fall of Adam and Eve, the human race, appearing to them in the guise of a serpent (Genesis 3:1–7). The Devil appeals to their pride to persuade men and women to reject God and follow their own selfish desires. Of the seven deadly sins, pride is the one most to be feared and so is to be especially assiduously avoided.

He has two other weapons which he deploys with great skill: first what might be termed 'self-kiddery' and, second, what I call 'safety in numbers'. It is not necessary to enlarge on the first: we all know how prone we are to it and each one of us can readily bring examples to mind. (Do we? Regularly? Are we fighting the fault?) The second is either when we are carried away as a member of a crowd, large or small, or are backed by a significantly large body of opinion; or when we are persuaded that, since everyone is doing something, it cannot be wrong. Indeed, a phenomenon of modern times is how huge masses can be assembled and manipulated by a determined individual, especially with the aid of television, to a

17 SATAN

point where their judgment becomes impaired or they act completely out of character. We are seeing Satan at work.

Sometimes bad behaviour is described as 'diabolical'. I wonder how many who use that word are aware that it means 'prompted by the Devil'?

Satan thrusts himself between man and God. He turns our mind from our relationship with God to a preoccupation with self, here and now and before all else. It is only allied to God that we can overcome him. We need God's grace.

Why is man so foolish as to prefer evil to good? To please himself rather than others? **'For I do not do the good I want, but the evil I do not want is what I do' (Romans 7:19). We must acknowledge that we can only blame ourselves.**

Since it is so important to build up a resistance to the Devil, and to encourage the committal to memory recommended in Chapter 6, I repeat here the prayer to St Michael:

'Holy Michael Archangel, defend us in the day of battle; be our safeguard against the wickedness and snares of the Devil. May God rebuke him, we humbly pray; and do thou Prince of the heavenly host, by the power of God, thrust down to Hell Satan and all wicked spirits who wander through the world for the ruin of souls. Amen.'

– Repeating prayers is an established tradition of the Catholic Church and the supreme example is the Rosary. Others are the '*Kyrie eleison*', the '*Agnus Dei*' and the '*Domine non sum dignus*' in a sung Mass in Latin. There are plenty more.

– Incidentally, Vatican II declared that the use of the Latin language is to be preserved in Latin rites. (*Constitution on the Latin Liturgy*, 4 December 1963.) Latin is also the language of the Church.

18

Sin

Pride is only one of seven deadly sins: the others are covetousness (avarice), lust, envy, gluttony, anger (wrath), and sloth (or acedia): (CCD 324 and, using the alternatives in brackets, CCC 1866.) How rarely do we hear of these? What do they each really mean? Are we keeping them in mind as we live our lives? They are 'the sources from which all other sins take their rise'. Naturally, there are seven contrary (directly opposing) virtues: humility, liberality, chastity, meekness, temperance, brotherly love and diligence. How often are these referred to by our pastors, and do we consciously practise them?

See how St Paul put it: '... do not gratify the desires of the flesh ... Now the works of the flesh are plain: fornication, impurity, licentiousness, idolatry, sorcery, enmity, strife, jealousy, anger, selfishness, dissension, party spirit, envy, drunkenness, carousing and the like ... But the fruit of the spirit is love, joy, peace, patience, kindness, goodness, faithfulness, gentleness, self-control; against such there is no law' (Galatians 5:16; 19–21; 22–3). (What does St Paul mean by 'party spirit'?)

Having written that first paragraph, it is necessary to take account of a welcome shift in the emphasis of the teaching of the Catholic Church on sin since Vatican II. Formerly based on more blunt ('Thou shalt not ...') prohibitions in the Ten Commandments – which have not changed – the Faithful are now encouraged to be more questioning in a responsible manner and more reliant on a well-informed conscience (see Chapter 41).

Well informed means being informed objectively under the light of the teaching of the Church, not subjectively, nor sentimentally, nor 'because it feels right'. To be well informed it is necessary to study and learn the teaching of the Church and to seek the advice of one's confessor. (Is this term still in use?) The 'don'ts'* continue to apply but we have been instructed that the reasons for them should be studied, clearly understood and kept in mind.

Sin is a personal act but others can cooperate in it in several ways, something often overlooked and worthy of informed reflection. **Sin is an act against God, against His law as taught by His Church, against one's neighbour, and it defiles one's integrity and that of the Mystical Body of Christ.** Sins are of commission or omission. They may be mortal or venial. All of them, like any infection, however small, affect the whole body: when I sin, I sin not only against God but against all the members of His Mystical Body, the Church. This is a reason for going to Confession (Chapter 15) which is often forgotten.

Only God can judge the sinner but sin and wrongdoing can and should be condemned because we love our neighbour. Wrong behaviour should not be shrugged off 'because that is how people behave these days', 'we must not upset them', or 'what can one do about it?'. Would that not be close to cooperation in the sins of others? This is a difficult question to answer but let us not lack courage and shirk it.

It is God Who will judge our minds and our actions in due course and we have been clearly told the dangers of sin to our immortal souls. Venial sin weakens and damages our will as well as our soul: mortal sin condemns the soul by defying God (see Chapter 24).

---

* The Latin for 'don't' is *noli*, literally 'do not want to'!

A combination of self-examination and meditation:

We have five senses: sight, hearing, taste, smell and touch. How does our use of each one square with the way Christ used it? For example, take sight: how would Jesus have regarded the same TV programmes, films, books, etc., which we have seen? What would He have looked at? What would He have shunned?

And so to examine and meditate upon our use of the other four senses.

To them can be added a faculty, speech. The ability to speak has probably been responsible for more unpleasantness, harm and evil than any other, and what we have said should bear the most rigorous examination and review. In contrast it can also be a force for the greatest good.

–No one is better fitted to guide and help us in the use of our senses than our guardian angel. The prayer quoted in Chapter 16 should be learnt by heart and said frequently.

How many of us can list from memory both the virtues and the capital sins? (I quoted them at the beginning of this chapter. There is a mnemonic to help us remember the latter: PALEGAS.) Note that these are all in the will and each is a positive choice. **Sin is always an assertion of self, putting self before God.**

There are six sins against the Holy Spirit listed in the 'Penny' Catechism (326). The list has not been repeated as such in the *Catechism of the Catholic Church*. Of course they remain sins and they are in it; see if you can find them there.

Do we know the four sins crying to Heaven for vengeance (CCD 327 and CCC 1867)? Look them up and ask yourself why those four were singled out. One of them is the sin of Sodom. I think a fifth, abortion, should be added, and that we should stand by with euthanasia for a sixth.

What we must remember about sin can be summed up in two sentences: sin damages and can eternally condemn our immortal soul; sin is defiance of God and it is He who is the Judge.

Redeemed

We are sinners. This is the result of Original Sin when Adam and Eve disobeyed God and fell from grace. The human race lost its supernatural life and condemned itself to mortality. Moreover, human nature was then flawed and became dominated by passion and imagination, both of which were to be exploited by Satan to make his conquests, leading people to eternal damnation with him.

But – and what a but! – God chose to redeem all mankind, a witness to His love for us and of our value. Not only that, He left a reliable guide and ongoing help, so that our flawed human nature need not fall again, or, having stumbled and strayed, is able to get back on track.

The guide and help are the Church He founded and the Sacraments given for its members (Chapters 9 and 15). While it is possible to save one's soul without Baptism, it will be much more difficult for those who are not baptised members of the Church with its fount of sanctifying grace. As significant for us to remember, however, is the ease with which Satan can and does knock down a soul, any soul, whether baptised or not. Did he not knock over the first Pope, Peter the Rock, who knew our Lord personally but still denied Him thrice? Another of Christ's chosen Apostles, Judas Iscariot, betrayed Him in return for money. Every day each of us offends God not once but seventy times seven times ...

Catholics may be cloaked with the Faith as well as having been redeemed, but unless we strive with every fibre of our being to do the Will of God and to strengthen ourselves with the grace of His Sacraments, we shall not be able to enter into His open, loving arms when we leave this life. Without His grace we are lost.

Mankind has been redeemed but we must claim the salvation of our souls by doing the Will of God. We shall only succeed through suffering, the taking up of our cross. **Only by yielding to the Will of God, martyrdom being the most ambitious sacrifice, can we find complete freedom and eternal happiness.** Our example is Jesus Christ Himself: His life on earth was for us, just to redeem us and guide us to share in His eternal life. As the sinners we are, we could not achieve this without His mercy and love.

'God, be merciful to me a sinner.' (The prayer of the tax collector in the temple – Luke 18:13.)
'Jesus, Mary and Joseph, I give you my heart and my soul.
'Jesus, Mary and Joseph, assist me in my last agony.
'Jesus, Mary and Joseph, may I die in peace, and in your blessed company.'
– These ejaculatory prayers have been favoured by many saints and can gain useful indulgences for the Holy Souls who have gone before us and will pray for us at our request. They can do so both in Purgatory and when they get to Heaven.

To end this chapter, let me propose an exercise. Your friend, a non-Christian, wakes up one last time from a fatal coma. He is bemused and recalls this story: that Jewish do-gooder with a train of followers in Israel who was lynched for desecrating the Temple, scourged and crucified last Friday, was reported to have been seen alive on Monday, his tomb empty, in the company of several of his closest associates. Your friend asks you more about this strange story. What will you tell him?

20

Our Purpose – Again

The purpose of this book was stated clearly in Chapter 1, but let me repeat it: to set down 'some of the essential tenets which I learnt at Ampleforth (1934–42), the casting-on stitches for a seamless cloak'. Also to be presented is a selection of 'short sections of the chain of linked teaching in their God-embracing contexts'. I expressed the hope that 'particularly contested issues, contraception for example, will be seen to fit naturally, be integral and easily acceptable'. Quite a challenge!

Sadly no illustrations can be provided, but readers have been encouraged to draw pictures in their minds. Not only will they serve to imprint the memory and make recall easier, but the imagination is constructively engaged and put out of reach of Satan, a tempter when we least expect him and who will strive to persuade the reader to selective – even indignant – dissent.

This would be a suitable place to pause and say again the prayer to the Holy Spirit (Chapter 1). It is one worth committing to memory. However, I shall put in its place the inspiring and beautiful Sequence said by all the Faithful at Mass on Pentecost Sunday:

> 'Holy Spirit, Lord of light
> From the clear celestial height
> > Thy pure beaming radiance give.
> Come, Thou Father of the poor,
> Come with treasures which endure
> > Come Thou light of all that live!

> Thou, of all consolers best,
> Thou, the soul's delightful guest,
> > Dost refreshing peace bestow;
> Thou in toil art comfort sweet;
> Pleasant coolness in the heat;
> > Solace in the midst of woe.
> Light immortal, light divine,
> Visit Thou these hearts of Thine,
> > And our inmost being fill:
> If Thou take Thy grace away,
> Nothing pure in man will stay;
> > All his good is turned to ill.
> Heal our wounds, our strength renew;
> On our dryness pour Thy dew;
> > Wash the stains of guilt away.
> Bend the stubborn heart and will;
> Melt the frozen, warm the chill;
> > Guide the steps that go astray.
> Thou, on us who evermore
> Thee confess and Thee adore,
> > With Thy sevenfold gifts descend:
> Give us comfort when we die;
> Give us life with Thee on high;
> > Give us joys that never die.'

– What a wonderful, all-embracing prayer! It is a prayer (why is it called 'Sequence'?) which most of us will not have fully appreciated as it is said quickly and in unison at Mass; and only once a year. Here is our chance to say it slowly, savouring the meaning of each phrase, meditating and rejoicing that it was written. Were someone to be taken hostage and placed in solitary confinement, to have

20 OUR PURPOSE - AGAIN

learnt this prayer before capture would be of enormous and continuing spiritual comfort.

✠

– Incidentally, do you know the sevenfold gifts of the Holy Spirit? They are: wisdom, understanding, counsel, fortitude, knowledge, piety and fear of the Lord (CCC 1830).
– Note the last-named: what does it mean and why is it one of these gifts? It is certainly much misunderstood and deserves our detailed study. As a starter, let me quote one expert. The fear of God is the beginning of wisdom, 'the fear being of all that is an offence against God' (*Crossing the Threshold of Hope,* Pope John Paul II). What others can you find?
– There are also twelve fruits of the Holy Spirit: charity, joy, peace, patience, kindness, goodness, generosity, gentleness, faithfulness, modesty, self-control and chastity (CCC 1832). Influenced by modernism, eight have been given undue priority – they are also humanist – while little attempt is made to grow and develop the last four. The principal victims of this neglect have been families and children: many have suffered grievously and permanently.

The Devil is shrewd, much cleverer than any of us, and we can learn from him. It is he, the Evil One, a real spirit, a fallen angel, who has targeted children, especially teenagers. By capturing their minds young he is able not only to enslave them to his wicked purpose but also to undermine the family. His successes are evident and widespread, headlined daily in the press all over the world. It is not the government, the police nor the social services but the Holy Spirit Who is our only defence. His gifts and fruits must be recognised, taught to our children, prayed for together and then cherished as precious jewels by daily practice. The Devil's influence can be banished by example, precept and prayer, yours and mine. 'Lord, in Thy mercy and love, please!'

21

The Creed

'I believe in one God ...' and '... in Jesus Christ ...'; 'I believe ... in the holy Catholic Church.' These words are taken from the Apostles' Creed, the '*Credo*' (Latin for 'I believe'). Transposed into Faith, they mean 'God made me', 'Jesus Christ redeemed me', and 'His Church is the way of my eternal salvation'. They are Articles of our Faith.

Have you drawn three descriptive pictures in your mind? Children can do this easily, but, sadly, it is more difficult as we grow older and get out of the practice. Close your eyes and use your imagination.

Before proceeding, let us pray the Apostles' Creed: 'I believe in God, the Father Almighty, Creator of Heaven and earth. I believe in Jesus Christ, his only Son, our Lord; He was conceived by the power of the Holy Spirit and born of the Virgin Mary. He suffered under Pontius Pilate, was crucified, died, and was buried. He descended to the dead. On the third day he rose again. He ascended into Heaven and is seated at the right hand of the Father. He will come again to judge the living and the dead. I believe in the Holy Spirit, the holy Catholic Church, the communion of saints, the forgiveness of sins, the resurrection of the body, and the life everlasting. Amen' (CCC 197).

✠

Do we truly mean all we say in the Creed? In particular, do we know what is meant by, for example, 'He descended to the

21 THE CREED

dead'? Or 'to judge the living and the dead'? Or 'the resurrection of the body'?

To deny one truth of our Faith is to deny the very foundation of the Faith itself - namely that Jesus Christ is God and that He founded the Church. To deny any dogma or traditional teaching of His Church is to deny that principle or foundation of Faith. This is the same as saying that God does not know the Truth or does not give us the Truth through the magisterium of the Church. Denial of any part of the authentic teaching of the Church is heresy, a grave sin*. A persistent heretic incurs a *latae sententiae* excommunication (Canon 1364).

The great Frank Sheed (see page 79) wrote in his book *The Church and I:* 'There is not as much difference as we might hope between the unbeliever who denies Christ's revelation and the believer who never gives his mind to it.' Now there is a thought to prick the conscience!

Here is another on which to ponder: 'To believe is to learn to think like God', from *Le Cavalier seul*, by André Frossard.

A Frenchman who led an extraordinary life (1915–95), André Frossard had a miraculous conversion from atheistic Marxism, survived Klaus Barbie's Montluc concentration camp and went on to become France's foremost social commentator and something of an icon. He became an intimate friend and confidant of Pope John Paul II. His daily, concise, witty and incisive reflections in *Le Figaro (Le Cavalier seul)* were eagerly sought, not least by me on frequent business trips to Paris, my favourite city, and his tenacity in regard to informing and guiding the secular culture through his Faith made him an example and inspiration for Catholics throughout the world.

Such men and women are put among us by God from time to time; we should look out for them and learn from their witness.

---

* In July 1998, Pope John Paul II issued *Ad Tuendam Fidem* (On the Defence of Faith), an apostolic letter directed at teachers and those in Catholic office. This is a most important directive confirming the fundamental teaching of the Church and it applies to all the Faithful. Buy it and read it. Disagreement, or refusal to accept what is taught in the *Catechism of the Catholic Church* (CCC), is heresy; wilful heretics deny themselves entry into the Kingdom of God, an eternal, personal catastrophe. Those who condone heresy place their souls at serious risk of the same fate.

22
The Two Great Commandments

Belief in God requires acceptance of His First Commandment: 'You shall love the Lord your God with your whole heart and your whole soul and your whole mind' (Matthew 22:37). Jesus describes it as 'the great and first commandment', and only a moment's contemplation is needed to show us why: He created us, He loves us and He keeps us in being; all we are and all we have we owe to Him. **Everything we have, including our lives, has been given to us by God on trust. Without Him we are nothing.**

The Second Commandment is: 'Love your neighbour as yourself' (Matthew 22:39).

Why? And who is my neighbour? Jesus gave His answer to the lawyer in the parable known as the Good Samaritan (Luke 10:29-37), but we have to look beyond that specific example.

Since God made each of us, and because He loves each and every one of us, therefore we are all 'neighbours'. We may not like many of them, or approve of what some of them do, or even know them, but we must love them as He does because He made them as He made us – in His own image and likeness.

This is a clear example of a short chain of linked teaching. Notice that sometimes uttered, at other times unspoken, there is always the additional welded link with God. One of the strengths of such a chain is that the answer to a question, for example: 'Must I love my enemy?', is there without it needing to be asked, clearly seen in the God-related context. Of course we must love our enemies, and our persecutors, and all wrongdoers, including the robbers of the Samaritan; they may be exercising their free will not

22 THE TWO GREAT COMMANDMENTS

to do His Will and commit evil, but He created them just as He created us, and He sustains their existence as He does ours. Therefore we must love and pray for all members of the human race without exception.

Moreover, if I am to obey the First Commandment, serving Him must include helping my neighbour, too, to do God's Will. Remember the Spiritual Works of Mercy? (See page 135) They comprise the second part of the awesome dual responsibility referred to in Chapters 1 and 6 which every Catholic must shoulder: the saving of my soul and the soul of my neighbour.

The two greatest commandments give us the life principle of all laws. Every law should respect the value of man: he is made in the image of God with an immortal soul which Christ redeemed by His death on the Cross. That is some value when you think about it! Every lawmaker must keep this in mind; also, that all authority comes from God.

By the way, do not be confused: the first two Commandments as quoted above were in the words of Jesus in the Gospel. When I quote the third, it will be in the words of God to Moses on Mount Sinai.

For the record, therefore, let me also quote the first two as they were given to Moses:

1. 'I am the Lord thy God, who brought thee out of the land of Egypt and out of the house of bondage. Thou shalt not have strange gods before Me. Thou shalt not make to thyself any graven thing; nor the likeness of anything that is in heaven above, or in the earth beneath, nor of those things that are in the waters under the earth. Thou shalt not adore them nor serve them' (Exodus 20:2–5).

2. 'Thou shalt not take the name of the Lord thy God in vain' (Exodus 20:7).

(The versions/translations in the *Catechism of the Catholic Church* differ slightly (CCC 2083–167). Why not compare them and consider what the reasons might be for the differences?)

Is not the First Commandment, especially, of first importance in today's world where man has so commonly elevated himself to be his own god, serving no one but himself? 'Egoistic man may have found himself at the head of the universe but one which has no meaning and in which man's life has no meaning' (*Society and Sanity*, F. J. Sheed).

Consider the death of a teenage son or daughter as a result of illness, accident or criminal assault, and try to explain it without reference to God; or how adequately to account for a loved one's agonising terminal cancer just in human terms? Understanding of the meaning of life rests only in Jesus Christ, Who is God and man.

Act of Faith:
'My God, I believe in Thee and all that Thy Church teaches because Thou hast said it and Thy word is true.'

Act of Hope:
'My God, I hope in Thee, for grace and for glory, because of Thy promises, Thy mercy and Thy power.'

Act of Charity:
'My God, because Thou art so good, I love Thee with all my heart, and for Thy sake, I love my neighbour as myself.'

A Simple Prayer Book, 1986 edition, CTS, London

– These will put a visa for entry to Paradise in your Christian passport, provided that you stamp it with an Act of Contrition (see page 80) at Confession.

23

Worshipping God

The Third Commandment is: 'Remember the Sabbath day, to keep it holy. Six days you shall labour, and do all your work; but the seventh day is a Sabbath to the Lord your God; in it you shall not do any work' (Exodus 20:8–10).

To rest from servile work is an important part of the Third Commandment. This is not so much a 'don't' – do not work – as a 'do' – do relax. Leisure is very necessary to well-being, health and culture, all of which we can see suffering, particularly as a result of shops being open on Sundays. Leisure is not the same as entertainment; it is time available for us to pursue our own interests, to relax, to see life as a whole and the world as a whole, thus fulfilling ourselves. We must beware lest we spend our leisure indulging in acquisitiveness, the 'getting and spending' against which William Wordsworth (English poet, 1770–1850) has warned and which has become the idol of our consumer society. It can become an addiction under the guise of 'retail therapy'.

Sadly, Sunday is now like any other day of the week and many have to work whether they wish to or not. This is one reason for the Church's ruling that the obligation to attend Sunday Mass may now be fulfilled on Saturday evening. This, however, is the only change in the attitude of the Church to the Sabbath. Look up the Third Commandment in the *Catechism of the Catholic Church* (CCC 2168–95).

Can I remain a member of any group if I am not behaving as it asks me to do, according to its rules, and actively participating in it? Sunday Mass, when we worship, praise and thank God, and offer ourselves humbly to Him, our loving Creator, is the central act of the Church; missing that must be an 'exclusive' act, one excluding oneself from the worship of God and from the other members of the group who obey the rules.

As we know, when travelling a difficult road on foot as one of a group, separation from our fellows can be dangerous, especially if we also lose our guide. To remind us of the peril of leaving the right road is one good reason why deliberately not going to Mass on Sunday, a holy day of obligation, is a mortal sin.

At Holy Mass, we not only go to God but He comes to us. At Holy Communion He comes into us. Should we not meet with Him more often than just on Sunday?

'Slow me down, Lord.
'Ease the pounding of my heart by the quieting of my mind. Steady my hurried pace with a vision of the eternal reach of time. Give me amid the confusion of the day, the calmness of the everlasting hills.
'Break the tension of my nerves and muscles with the soothing music of the singing streams that live in my memory. Help me to know the restoring power of sleep.
'Teach me the art of taking minute vacations – of slowing down to look at a flower, to chat with a friend, to pat a dog, to read a few lines from a good book.
'Slow me down, Lord, and inspire me to send my roots deep into the soil of life's enduring values that I may grow towards the stars of my great destiny.'

Cardinal Richard Cushing, 1895–1970
Archbishop of Boston, 1944–70

– Especially on the Sabbath, say this prayer and practise what you are requesting. Then listen; the Lord will speak to you.

23 WORSHIPPING GOD

The Mass is the great central act of worship of the Church. 'To me nothing is so consoling, so piercing, so thrilling, so overwhelming as the Mass ... the greatest action that can be on earth.' I have quoted Cardinal Newman. What is our own view? Do we really understand what is meant by 'the holy sacrifice of the Mass'? More particularly, have we read about and studied 'the Sacred Mysteries', and how we should participate in the celebration of the Mass?

A reminder: contrary to widespread belief, the traditional Mass of the Roman Missal, incorrectly referred to as the Tridentine Mass, which was the Holy Mass said in Latin throughout the Church for hundreds of years prior to Vatican II, is still an essential part of the Catholic liturgy. Indeed, it should be more available to the Faithful and more frequent, by reason of the *Ecclesia Dei motu proprio* of the Pope to the bishops of the world in July 1988.

At Pentecost every year, there is a pilgrimage from Notre Dame in Paris to the magnificent medieval cathedral at Chartres which begins and ends with traditional High Mass. En route there are all-night Expositions of the Blessed Sacrament and Confessions. Already huge, it is attracting increasing numbers from many countries, and has a particular appeal for young people who have not before attended services in the Roman rite. What lessons can be learnt from seeing so many drawn to worship and penance by the traditional Latin liturgy, especially when parish congregations and the numbers going to Confession are in decline? May the Holy Spirit descend again in 'tongues as of fire' (Acts 2:3) to direct us.

One more thought: to love God is to worship Him, which requires affirmative action. Moreover, love is not a permit for an own code of moral conduct. **We must go to Mass and keep His commandments on pain of sin. In particular expect not to be popular and pray that God will not ask you to accept martyrdom. Be sure, however, that each of us will suffer for His sake.**

77

24

Mortal Sin

A mortal sin, like quite deliberately refusing to go to Mass on Sunday (CCC 2181), is an act of defiance of God. My will is turned against His; the teaching of His Church is disobeyed, thereby condemning His Word. A mortal sin is an act of pride and rebellion, a turning away from God. It may be doing what God has forbidden (sin of commission) or failing to do what He has commanded (sin of omission). The defiance may be not only in our words and actions but also in our innermost thoughts and desires. Moreover, as we have noted (Chapter 18), any sin does harm to the Mystical Body of the Church and should be avoided at all costs.

A mortal sin has to be absolved by a priest in Confession, and we are bound by the Second and Third Precepts of the Church to go to Confession and receive the Blessed Sacrament in Holy Communion, the Eucharist, at least once a year (CCC 2041).

Three conditions are necessary for a sin to be mortal: grave matter, full knowledge and complete consent. With regard to grave matter, we must be guided by the Ten Commandments; they should not only be known but also their full meaning understood. In particular, we should try to find out through study the reason why any forbidden thought or act is an offence against God or our neighbour. Complete consent means deliberately choosing the evil. On occasion the decision may not have been followed by the doing of the wrong; the sin, however, will have been committed by the expressed intention to commit it.

'Mortal sin exists also when a person knowingly and willingly, for whatever reason, chooses something gravely disordered' (*Veritatis Splendor*'). This must be taken into account where an end is used to justify a means. Think of some examples. One is quoted in the fifth paragraph of Chapter 32 (page 108).

24 MORTAL SIN

Which of us has not found to our cost that when we took the first seemingly innocent step on the downward slope, we persuaded ourselves that we had done nothing wrong? Which of us could have suspected at the time that we had broken down the barriers and cleared the way for sin?

In the garden of Eden, the man blamed the woman and she blamed the serpent. Certainly he was tempted by her and she by the serpent, but it was his decision, and hers, to yield to the temptation.

Why do we sin? In the crisp words of Frank Sheed: 'Because we damn well choose to!'

(Quoted several times already, Frank Sheed, an Australian born in 1896, graduated with first-class honours in Latin, French and English at Sydney University and then read Law. Coming to England, he worked full-time for the Catholic Evidence Guild for four years. He considered this experience of inestimable value and spoke on CEG platforms for the rest of his life. With his wife, Maisie Ward, he founded the publishing firm, Sheed & Ward, in both London and New York. As author and public speaker, as publisher, editor and translator, his major contribution was to bring about the revival of Catholic scholarship and theology throughout the English-speaking world. Two of his books on theology – see the Book List – are particularly recommended.)

A common impulsion to sin is drink: alcohol excites an ego and fuddles a conscience. We must watch our consumption at all times, but especially where occasions of mortal sin may be lurking. In particular, driving becomes

dangerous after a drink – and sinful too (CCC 2290).

Although sin is a personal act, we have to be careful not to cooperate in sins committed by others (Chapter 18). Especially must we be wary of being carried along by fashionable opinion or general conduct contrary to the teaching of the Church. Not only shall we be sinning but also blunting our resistance, and making it easier to slip into serious wrongdoing and so to offend the goodness of our loving God; we shall be on the slope to Hell.

An Act of Contrition is essential for our journey:
'O my God, I am heartily sorry for having offended Thee because Thou art so good and sin displeases Thee, and I firmly resolve with the help of Thy grace never to offend Thee again.'
– Note the use of the pronouns Thou, Thee and Thy. They continue to be common in the prayers of the Church, but not with any apparent consistency in new English translations. Their use has been the traditional practice in Latin, the official language of the Church; also in French, from which the *Catechism of the Catholic Church* was translated into English, and in many other languages.
– I have also used the capital letter where the pronoun refers to God, He Who is above all and unique.
– **Have you bowed your head every time you read the name Jesus?**

✠

At Fatima on 13 July 1917 it was on little Jacinta that the vision of Hell had the greatest impact: 'a terrifying sight and sound of millions of lost souls'.

On 10 December 1975 at Pontevedra, the Bishop of Fatima had this to say: 'In the light of the Fatima message, sin is not a phenomenon of the social order, but is, in the true theological concept, an offence against God with necessary social consequences. Perhaps in no other century has life been so sinful. But there is something new added to the sins of this century: the man of today, more sinful than those who came before him, has lost the sense of sin ... Man of today has arrived at this stage because he has placed

24 MORTAL SIN

a division between himself and God ... believing that when God is ignored, everything is possible. The man of this century wishes to realise himself as stronger than God and against God, and comes finally to the point of man debased, anti-man, because man can only perfectly realise himself in God.' The alternative is Hell.

Do you know exactly what was the message of Our Lady at Fatima? Are you aware that it was accompanied by the most momentous event since the Resurrection? The miracle of the sun was seen by huge numbers, believers and unbelievers alike. Be sure that we shall ignore at our peril what Our Lady specifically besought at Fatima of each one of us.

Two books on Fatima are recommended in the Book List.

Let me now take the opportunity to introduce G. K. Chesterton (see the Epilogue):

'The Fall is a view of life. It is not the enlightening, but the only encouraging view of life. It holds ... that we have misused a good world and not merely been trapped in a bad one. It refers evil back to a wrong use of the will, and thus declares that it can eventually be righted by the right use of the will. Every other creed except that one is some form of surrender to fate.'

The Thing, 1957 edition

There are, therefore, objective standards of goodness which rely on the natural law, the divine law and the grace of God. In order to know them, and choose them, we must study the teaching of the Church and learn to pray (see Chapters 42 and 43).

A final thought: 'In a world without God, life is absurd.' André Malraux, French philosopher and politician (1901-76). To which let me add 'A world without God is a world without hope' (Cardinal Joseph Ratzinger) and 'To seek peace without God is an absurdity' (Pope St Pius X 1903-14).

Well, isn't it?

Read again the passage from Wisdom on page 5.

25

Penance and Fasting

To strengthen our resolve and to encourage the practice of prayer, of works of charity and self-denial, the pre-Vatican II Second Commandment of the Church bound us to observe the appointed days of penance. These were each Friday of the year and the season of Lent. They were to be devoted to the disciplining of self.

In the *Catechism of the Catholic Church* the six Commandments of the Church have been reduced to five and called Precepts, avoiding the earlier confusion between the two sets of Commandments. The old Sixth Commandment, providing for the material needs of the Church, has become 'a duty' (CCC 2041–3). The explanations of each in Chapter V of the 'Penny' Catechism have not been included.

Since the great Council of Pope John XXIII, emphasis on the penance of fasting and abstinence has been lightened. The new guidelines for fasting and penance on Fridays (Statement from the Bishops of England and Wales on Canon 1249–53) are not so well known. (Do you know them?) Moreover, the traditional link between prayer and fasting appears to be less visible. Is this one reason why sinning has become more frequent and widespread, sinning which is increasingly not acknowledged as such by rationalising consciences under the manipulation of the Devil? Satan has also been extremely successful in making us immune to feelings of guilt and shame, often putting in its place as the only criterion what we can justify to ourselves or get away with.

Christ teaches that we all have a cross to bear, that we shall all suffer for His sake as He suffered for us. Fasting and abstinence are essential training exercises to prepare us for these trials.

25 PENANCE AND FASTING

'Behold, O good and most sweet Jesus, I cast myself upon my knees in Thy sight, and with the most fervent desire of my soul, I pray and beseech Thee that Thou wouldst impress upon my heart lively sentiments of Faith, Hope and Charity, with true repentance for my sins and a firm purpose of amendment, whilst with deep affection and grief of soul, I ponder within myself and mentally contemplate Thy five most Precious Wounds, having before my eyes that which David spoke in prophecy of Thee, O good Jesus, "They have pierced My hands and My feet, they have numbered all My bones" '(Psalm 22:16–17).

– **There are 150 Psalms from which to choose other prayers.**
– An invocation said three times in the traditional Mass combines humility and faith: 'Lord, I am not worthy that Thou shouldst enter under my roof; but only say the word, and my soul will be healed.'

✠

The harm done by venial sins is too often overlooked. Because we are all members of Christ's Mystical Body, any evil - every sin offends God and is evil - which we inflict on ourselves and, therefore, on His Mystical Body, affects us all. Moreover, as any lapse in training reduces competitive performance, so the venial sins we commit weaken us spiritually and make us less resistant to a temptation to mortal sin.

Purgatory exists to cleanse souls from the stains of venial sin. Remembering the unimaginable suffering of Jesus to redeem us from sin, the experience will be extremely painful and should be avoided at all costs. Venial sin is not to be condoned.

You may now be inclined to find out more about plenary indulgences and how to gain them (see Chapter 26).

26

Purgatory

While repentance and Sacramental Absolution obtain forgiveness of sin, and get the soul back on track with a generous gift of grace, sin leaves disfiguring marks and stains which will require some painful 'atonement' to remove.

It is worth finding out the meaning and origin of the word atonement. It would be a gainful little exercise.

When invited to the home of a friend, if our only clothing is soiled, shall we not be eager to wash it before crossing the threshold? (Do you remember the parable of the wedding feast in the Gospel (Matthew 22:1–14)? A guest who did not put on a (clean) wedding garment was punished – very severely indeed.) Our soul must be pure and without stain of sin in order to enter the presence of God.

The washing of the soul on our pilgrimage on earth is accomplished through the miraculous Sacrament of Penance, but the deep sin stains on it must be removed in Purgatory after death, to make us worthy to enjoy God's eternal love. It is punishment which we will have brought on ourselves and thoroughly deserve. We have offended God, and we shall want to make retribution before we can feel worthy to enter His presence. A clean garment will take the place of our trusty seamless knitted cloak.

We can help the souls in Purgatory by praying for them.

'O my God, have mercy on the poor souls in Purgatory. Put an end to their sufferings and bring them to eternal life. Through the same Christ our Lord.'

26 PURGATORY

– Never forget them. Remember also that when they get to Heaven, the Holy Souls can intercede directly with God for us; in the meantime they can pray to Him for us now.

– We can also gain indulgences for the Holy Souls as well as for ourselves (CCC 1471–9). These can remit part or even all punishment in Purgatory, a wonderful gift in our keeping. We need to learn the conditions on which indulgences are granted and go for them, both for the Holy Souls and for ourselves. They may be found in *A Simple Prayer Book*, Catholic Truth Society, 1986 edition, pages 44–5.

When you pray for the souls in Purgatory, which should be at least a twice-daily habit, morning and night, remember especially all those who have no one else to pray for them.

See the prayer on the inside back cover

☦

As we approach the time of our death – of course we never know how close we are – then provided we are in a state of grace, i.e. not under the shroud of a mortal sin (see Chapter 24) we can be pretty sure that after our judgment (see Chapters 12 and 13), we shall immediately find ourselves in Purgatory. With this thought in mind I can give you a poem by a renowned Farm Street Jesuit I came across a while back, which will bring this chapter to an appropriate end.

Christ, when the lamp of life is burning low
And shadows thicken round us – at the end
We shall remember that we called Thee friend,
And heard Thee speaking with us on the way:
So at Thy call, naught fearing, we shall go
Out of the darkness to the perfect day.

Fr R. H. J. Steuart SJ, 1874–1948

27

The Sacraments

God is more than our Father and our friend. He made us and keeps us in being and loves us. Nothing that we could do for Him, therefore, would be enough; indeed, even our uttermost could only be minuscule. This is a daunting thought, but He has provided a way to enable us to please Him. Not only did He send His Son to redeem mankind – who suffered and died on the Cross for us, for you, dear reader – but His Son, Jesus Christ, founded a Church to teach us His Way and to administer the seven Sacraments which He gave us (CCD 249–55 and CCC 1210–1690).

Three have already been referred to: Baptism, the Eucharist (Holy Communion), and Penance & Reconciliation (Confession). What are the other four? Confirmation, Anointing of the Sick, Holy Orders and Matrimony. They deserve serious attention but I propose to leave all but one, Matrimony (see Chapter 28), for you to look up and study in some of the books listed. In particular, note that the confirmed person 'receives the power to profess faith in Christ publicly and as it were officially (*quasi ex officio)*' (CCC 1285 and St Thomas Aquinas).

Can you remember when and where, and by whom, you were confirmed? what name(s) did you take? More importantly, can you recall why you were confirmed?

God has guaranteed that whatever we want to do to please Him, He will help us do. We have only to ask, as most of us do twice daily, on our knees every morning and night, when we say in the '*Pater*

27 THE SACRAMENTS

Noster', the 'Our Father': 'Thy Will be done'. But do we always realise the meaning of what we are praying? Do we remind ouselves that Jesus Himself gave us this prayer during His Sermon on the Mount? (Matthew 6:9-13) What a unique, personal gift!

Let us say the Lord's Prayer now, very slowly, thinking carefully about what we are saying:

> 'Our Father, Who art in Heaven, hallowed be Thy name, Thy kingdom come, Thy Will be done on earth as it is in Heaven. Give us this day our daily bread, and forgive us our trespasses, as we forgive those who trespass against us, and lead us not into temptation, but deliver us from evil. Amen.'

– When did you last read this prayer off a printed page? When did you last savour each phrase and all that it means? Why not do it tomorrow after you wake, before you get up out of bed and kneel down to say your offertory and morning prayers?

–Try to imagine, too, what God might say to you during pauses between the phrases.

–Wake up to God! Listen to Him. Deliver us from the evil one.

☩

I trust that we have not got this far together without my having made the point that any study I have undertaken is no substitute for your own studious application. Thoroughly to understand the teaching of the Church is a DIY job, especially post-Vatican II. (There is a sound reason for adding these four words: find out what it is. Go to the Documents of the Council which have been read by far too few at all levels in the Church.) All of us must seek the Truth and bear witness to it, a lifelong responsibility whose discharge will determine our eternal future.

I am aware that there are several small imperfections in my witness of the Truth in this book. Please forgive them. In defence I offer these words:"Nothing would be done at all if a man waited till he could do it so well that no one could find fault with it." I have quoted John Henry, Cardinal Newman (See p. 124)

28

Holy Matrimony

There is one area of human behaviour where the moral conflict, right versus wrong, is most acute. This is the area of our sexual conduct, and it is covered by the next of the Ten Commandments to be considered, the Sixth: 'Thou shalt not commit adultery' (Exodus 20:14; Deuteronomy 5:18; CCD 209-13; CCC 2331-400 which takes up twelve pages). Like most of the Commandments, the meaning of the words is clear, but have we thought out why adultery – and fornication by unmarried men and women – is forbidden? Have we framed the context? Do we see their links in the chain of God's teaching?

The Sixth is not the only Commandment ruling the attitude and behaviour of man in his sexual conduct. The Ninth states: 'Thou shalt not covet thy neighbour's wife' (Deuteronomy 5:21; CCD 223-5). Nor thy neighbour's husband, of course.

In the *Catechism of the Catholic Church* this Ninth Commandment is expressed as follows: 'You shall not covet your neighbour's house; you shall not covet your neighbour's wife, or his manservant, or his maidservant, or his ox, or his ass, or anything that is your neighbour's.' These words are taken from Exodus, a deliberate tie-up with tradition. (CCC 2514-33 – three more pages to the twelve for the Sixth.) It adds: 'Everyone who looks at a woman lustfully has already committed adultery with her in his heart' (Matthew 5:28). How many of us, men and women, take ourselves to task on this account, including when watching television or at a cinema?

I think it is worth completing the passage in the Gospel referred to above. It comes from Jesus in His Sermon on the Mount:

28 HOLY MATRIMONY

'If your right eye causes you to sin, pluck it out and throw it away: it is better that you lose one of your members than your whole body be thrown into Hell' (Matthew 5:29). These are very strong words: ask yourself, why did Jesus use them?

When a man and woman decide to marry, the prime objective is to start a family. Had not God blessed Adam and Eve and said, 'Be fruitful and multiply' (Genesis 1:28)? Adding emphasis, the Church states in Canon Law 1085 that any inability to have sexual intercourse invalidates marriage, a state endowed by God with its own proper laws. We can see why. 'The well-being of the individual person and of both human and Christian society is closely bound up with the healthy state of conjugal and family life' (*'Gaudium et Spes'*). **The married state is an intimate communion of life and love established by God, not by man.**

This state is entered through the Sacrament of Matrimony (CCD 306–12 and CCC 1601–66). The man and the woman make certain indissoluble promises to each other before witnesses and, joined together into one flesh, are blessed with God's grace, immediately and in their future life together. Married couples enjoy the advantages and contentment of their loving, lifelong commitment to each other: the satisfaction of their mutual giving of each other without reserve, and the joy of their intimate physical union.

Marriage, therefore, despite the romance and the ceremonial panoply with which it is usually associated is a solemn, binding contract. (This is more obvious in the case of arranged marriages. These, incidentally, prove themselves less likely to end in divorce than where falling in love is the signal for a wedding.) Voluntarily entered into with full knowledge, marriage is a commitment which will not be easy to deliver and will have many ups and downs. Marriage is a practical arrangement of living together by a man and a woman; there are rules and it is intended to endure, as is made clear in the vows made by the couple to each other – 'till death us do part' – at their wedding.

It is the firm, undisputed teaching of the Church that 'what God has joined together', a valid marriage blessed by the Church, 'let no man put asunder'(Matthew 19:6). If a marriage can be proved not to have been valid, an annulment may be possible and there are formal procedures to consider this, but there can be no divorce. A valid marriage is indissoluble. It is up to the pair, who freely commit themselves to each other, lovingly to work it out to the end, come what may. God will give them the grace to do so.

In extreme circumstances, a couple may separate and live apart. They may seek a civil divorce. They will, however, remain indissolubly married to each other. Should either wed again – this can only be a legal arrangement which is formally registered – they must remain celibate or they will be committing adultery, thus choosing to cut themselves off from the Sacraments of the Church.

Adultery is an offence against God, Who blesses a valid marriage. It is also an offence against the innocent spouse who is doubly cheated: by the adulterer, who commits a breach of promise, and by the adulterer's victim, who becomes a thief, stealing something that belongs to another. Specifically forbidden by the Sixth Commandment, fornication is also theft, stealing the pleasure that rightly belongs only within marriage. There are no obvious circumstances in which these two acts would not be mortal sins.

'Mary and Joseph, we pray to you that God, our Almighty Father, will preserve and strengthen the institution of marriage throughout the world, and give all those who commit themselves to it in loving union for life, the grace to remain faithful and bring each other to eternal happiness in Heaven.'

✠

Male and Female

After puberty, boys and girls become young men and women – but not yet responsible adults – endowed by Almighty God with the power of procreation. They possess organs with a unique, complementary, reproductive function which can be exercised in a coital act which He, our loving Creator, may decide to bless with a conception, the gift of a soul in His creation of a new life in the womb of the woman. Not every act does result in the generation of life, but that is its purpose.

It should be appreciated that if human beings were not meant to have children, their reproductive organs, male and female, so complex and yet so delicate, designed by God for the marriage act, would not be there at all. Inspired by Him, the Catholic Church understandably teaches reverence for this unique, wonderful faculty and She considers its use sacred.

Human beings have been given two appetites, hunger and thirst. After puberty they also experience sexual desire. The two appetites must be heeded: food and water are required to keep us alive. Sexual desire, also a gift of God, is designed to ensure procreation of the human race. It is not an appetite. Nor is it a drive, irresistible and/or uncontrollable, whose satisfaction is essential to happiness or even well-being. In fact, we have many natural desires, some of which are not pleasant at best and are illegal at worst; we control, or abstain from, all of them for the good of others and for our own good. Unlike animals which act instinctively, we have the faculty of self-control.

The restraint of sexual desire for any length of time, even its complete denial, is not at all harmful. On the contrary, despite the torrent of promotion of sexual indulgence as natural and right, and despite the widespread scorn for virginity, both chastity and sexual abstinence have clearly proved beneficial, not only spiritually but also with regard to a person's well-being and health. Marooned on a desert island, alone without food and water, one might ail and die of starvation and thirst, but certainly not from sexual continence.

Contrary to popular opinion, sexual desire is not an appetite which has to be satisfied by sexual activity. Nor is it a compulsion: we are not animals with no more control than their instincts; we are men and women with free will who can exercise self-control and abstinence. **It is a fact that in order to achieve our potential in whatever we undertake, we must discipline ourselves to the point of self-denial.** (Think hard about this statement for a few minutes. It has very wide application.)

The wish to indulge in sexual activity by a single person is prompted by desire. This is a natural, normal physical longing. However, it cannot be interpreted, let alone translated into action, and will soon subside, if the person experiencing it knows nothing about how the sexual organs function. Nor can it be fulfilled if circumstances do not permit. These are two aspects which used to be preached and practised. Innocence and conventional elimination of opportunity – providing chaperones, for example, or insisting on modest dress and behaviour and language – were bastions against sexual licence. A table between people also shielded many from temptations to immoral behaviour; this applied especially to meetings in presbytery, parlour, office and surgery. Even where a coffee was accepted after an evening out.

Sexual desire, then, is a natural longing which strikes one's body often unexpectedly. It is transient, unless encouraged by wishing or mental fantasies, and subsides as quickly as it arises. It can be ignored; it can also be overcome by a decisive distraction.

29 MALE AND FEMALE

('Healthy pursuits' used frequently to be recommended in my young days.) It is not an urge which must be satisfied, a fact clearly demonstrated daily by the behaviour of the majority of boys and girls, men and women, in everyday living, and even by couples in their married life.

Although there are tragic exceptions, is it not remarkable how members of families – brothers and sisters, step-siblings, adopted children and cousins, not to mention parents and their children, or aunts and uncles and their nephews and nieces – normally never engage in sexual activity or regard each other as objects of sexual desire? What stops them? Why does such activity become acceptable in today's world if it is with someone else's brother or sister, with an unrelated daughter or son?

Did you know – I only found out recently by a happy chance – that in Jesus' day, boys and girls after the age of puberty and before betrothal or marriage addressed each other as brother and sister? Chastity before marriage was preached and practised.

Sexual desire is a gift of God, and if we have the right attitude and the will, we can keep it under proper restraint and benefit thereby.

He understands our weakness and the pressure of hedonism in the world, how our will can be undermined, and He will give us the grace to stand firm when we ask for it. Moreover, is not His love, now and for ever, to be preferred to transient sexual pleasure?

'Christ, my Lord, help me to develop the strength I need to be chaste in thought, word and deed. Help me to keep aware of Thy presence: then I shall not offend Thee so easily. Grant me a healthy distrust of myself and that I acknowledge my feebleness. Prevent me, dear Jesus, from kidding myself that strict chastity is asking too much. Keep me pure in body and spirit, that I may be welcome in Thy Kingdom.

'May Thy Blessed Mother, Mary, pray for me that I may always be proud to have her watching me in all I do.'

✠

An aphorism for unmarried young people: it is not a love life but a love of life with friends which leads to contentment (see Chapter 31).

Women yearn to be treated with chaste respect, and one of their shining qualities is the virtue of modesty. In this they differ from men, who are generally more competitive, crude and macho, a trait encouraged by consumerism. However, led by a strident feminist lobby, women have been persuaded to be more assertive, to isolate 'sex' from its true purpose and function, and to claim sexual equality. Thus they put at risk their natural role of living in chaste, complementary harmony as sisters with considerate brothers, until marrying in due course and having children.

To claim that women are the same as, meaning equal to, men, sexually or otherwise, is to fly in the face of the facts. Nor is it in their interest. Even the opportunities open to a woman – this applies especially to a wife and mother – can never be completely equal, whatever legislation says. Neither are men equal to each other. Each man and woman, a unique, incomparable creation of God, each with different gifts, must rely, hopefully without facing any prejudice, on their intelligence, skills, character, motivation, physical aptitude and availability, and will progress accordingly. Or not – because not all is fair in a world peopled with sinners.

Men and women, male and female, are not the same. We have God to thank for that (Genesis 1:27). He also created us for eternal life with Him. These are realities; to ignore them is to distort the truth and to raise false materialist goals for our journey on earth.

30

Sexual Conduct

Anthropological history shows that it has been natural practice, commonly taught and generally accepted since the human race was created, that sexual activity has been strictly controlled, sometimes even proscribed, in the interest of harmonious living in communities. This is a feature in the conventions and customs of all the world's early communities, and every nation today has a legal code of practice governing sexual conduct. It may not be comprehensive in each case, but always marriage is regulated.

Despite such formal control, sexual licence has erupted from time to time and led to depravity and destruction, in communities, in families and in individuals, both men and women. This is a result of the suppression of almost all reference to our reproductive faculty, the unique function of the sexual organs being to beget children, except to ensure that it is thwarted in the pursuit of sexual pleasure.

The Devil's success in promoting sexual licence, the indulgence of lust, is alarming. Satan has established the general view in society, or a lame acquiescence to it, that everyone has the right to sexual gratification in whatever manner it can legitimately be achieved as soon as boys and girls are pubescent. Most have no hesitation or difficulty in becoming 'sexually active' in their teens, the availability of the pill breaking down the natural reserve and apprehension of women and girls. Predatory men are encouraged by the knowledge that women are prepared to yield their bodies for sexual pleasure, however selectively, and those men who do not have all the gratification they desire resort to sexual harassment, assault, rape and incest. This is increasing, and even children and the very old, not strong enough to defend themselves, are now frequent victims of vicious sexual assault. The perpetrators of these ghastly crimes include quite young boys.

There has been a parallel and outspoken increase in homosexual and lesbian sexual activity, neither permitted by God, and whose genital acts are an abuse of natural functions.

The outbreak of Aids, as well as the increase in other sexually transmitted diseases, was an unexpected setback to Satan's progress but he has skilfully countered it with his 'safe sex' campaign. The slogan translates: carry on having sex, everybody; just make it safe by using a condom. Such diabolical cunning! The right way to avoid Aids is of course to obey the Sixth Commandment.

The word 'sex' originally meant 'gender', but it has come to be used generally for any sexual activity and allusion to it, not just natural sexual intercourse. The 'sex cocktail', to coin a term, is now ubiquitously employed commercially and, seemingly, with a profitable return. It is used to spice books and sell them. Fornication and adultery are common – even indispensable – themes on screen and stage, often explicitly enacted to lure audiences, playing on their weakness for prurience and voyeurism. (Say a prayer for the actresses and actors who have to prostitute themselves in the lewd scenes demanded by directors.) Newspapers are never without a sex-linked item. Holidays are organised for sex. Sex is used to warp the young and push them towards drug addiction. Pornography is spreading as fast as the romantic can be made salacious, developed into 'soft porn', a euphemism to make it seem harmless, and then blatantly turned into 'hard pornography'. Computers are a new outlet for this degradation of people.

Notice how mammary glands, whose purpose is to suckle babies, have been turned into a fashion accessory, moneymaker and fetish. The shy breasts of women are shamelessly featured by, and have become a source of profit to, couturiers, outerwear and underwear manufacturers, jewellers, tabloid newspapers,

30 SEXUAL CONDUCT

impresarios, photographers, dieticians and cosmetic surgeons. Ironically, many mothers have to be persuaded to breast-feed their newborn babies rather than give them a bottle.

The male organ, too, is emerging as a productive source of profit: for photographers, sex therapists and cosmetic surgeons. What next?

Satan's 'sexual bait', to coin another term, is hooking many, many men and women, boys and girls, and, tragically, hundreds of priests; he must be waiting gleefully in Hell to welcome their souls to eternal damnation. He has established concupiscence as a latter-day golden calf (Exodus 32:1–14).

It does not stop at that: there is a growing portrayal of unspeakable sexual depravity and cruelty on film and video which is increasingly translated into practice, as shown up in crime statistics and media reports. The outlook is grim.

Premarital sex started the rot. Its incidence rapidly increased and earned grudging tolerance before becoming accepted. Permissiveness spread to extramarital sex. **Sexual organs are now being stimulated and exercised in a manner and with a frequency which not even animals practise and has nothing to do with procreation.** It is called being 'sexually active' and is widely regarded as a normal, pleasurable pastime, thereby trivialising all sexual relationships and releasing them from any code of morals.

Those who introduced mixed university accommodation, the suppliers of free contraceptives and confidential advice, and parents who turned a blind eye to the sexual conduct of their sons and daughters have much to answer for. So, too, does the teaching profession. And our bishops and priests: their welcome for 'Humanae Vitae', so deserved by a gentle, kind and prophetic papal letter to the Faithful (have you read it?), was drowned by criticism, much of it from within the Church; the teaching of the encyclical is not so loud or clear as the campaign to allow conscience to overrule many of its precepts. What has happened since *'Veritatis Splendor'* was issued by Pope John Paul II to the bishops of the world, whose first task, quoting from *'Lumen Gentium'*, is to be the authentic teachers of the apostolic Faith?

Immoral sexual conduct is probably not as widespread as many fear, but who can deny the serious harm it is wreaking on society, families, children and many, many individuals?

How many marriages in Britain break down and end in divorce? One in two or three? Statistically the likelihood of such breakdown is at least twice as great where either party has indulged in premarital sex. This is not commonly known and has perhaps been deliberately concealed. Divorce is big business, not only for lawyers but for many other people.

'My son, if you receive my words and treasure up my commandments within you;
Making your ear attentive to wisdom and inclining your heart to understanding;
Yes, if you cry out for insight and raise your voice for understanding;
If you seek it like silver and search for it as for hidden treasures;
Then you will understand the fear of the LORD and find the knowledge of God;
For the LORD gives wisdom; from His mouth come knowledge and understanding;
He stores up sound wisdom for the upright; He is a shield to those who walk in integrity,
Guarding the paths of justice and preserving the way of His saints;
Then you will understand righteousness and justice and equity, every good path;

30 SEXUAL CONDUCT

'For wisdom will come into your heart, and knowledge will be pleasant to your soul;
Discretion will watch over you; understanding will guard you;
Delivering you from the way of evil, from men of perverted speech,
Who forsake the paths of uprightness to walk in the ways of darkness,
Who rejoice in doing evil and delight in the perverseness of evil;
Men whose paths are crooked, and who are devious in their ways.'

From the twentieth book of the Old Testament, an extract from one of thirty-one Proverbs (2:1–15). It was written specifically for young people by Solomon, son of David, King of Israel.

'Dear Jesus, who enjoined Thy disciples to be "wise as serpents" (Matthew 10:16), direct all eyes to the Proverbs whose positive and negative standards provide a valuable test of personal conduct. In Thy mercy, Lord, grant them the grace to understand and observe Thy wisdom.'

✠

A Note

The first surveys of sexual conduct were those of Kinsey (1948 and 1953) and Masters & Johnson (1966) in America. They created a sensation at the time, not only for daring to expose such an intimate area of human behaviour but also because of the startling practices that were revealed. Released with maximum publicity and exploited demoniacally, these studies were the beginning of the sex industry, and the extent of its malign influence has been incalculable. Standards of sexual practice were preached, and those who did not conform were deemed not normal. Man's and woman's sexual faculty was detached from its procreative function and became just a means of achieving sensual pleasure, supposedly the right of every person as soon as puberty had been reached. Sexual drive, hormones and individual desires were all that mattered.

Sponsored among others by the US Government, prompted by the need for accurate data to assist in the battle against Aids, a new survey, comprehensive and methodologically sound, was published in 1995: *Sex in America* by Robert Michael, John H. Gagnon, Edward O. Laumann and Gina Kolata, based on the National Health and Social Life Survey (NHSLS). It reached two important conclusions. First, that the vast majority of previous studies were unreliable and many worse than useless; they were deeply flawed. Second, and this is borne out by the data established, 'Sexual behaviour is shaped by our social surroundings. We behave the way we do, we even desire what we do, under the strong influence of the particular social groups we belong to. We do not have all the latitude we may imagine ...' America is not a nation of sex maniacs, and the majority of people enter and remain in long-term relationships. Granted there are exceptions, as might be expected in view of our wilful natures: chastity before marriage is not always honoured, there are extramarital affairs and divorce is widespread. Normal behaviour, however, conforms closely to what sensible people might expect.

It seems to me that the common practice revealed – and why should it only be found in the USA? – also conforms closely to just what is taught by the Catholic Church.[*] Isn't that an actuality of fundamental significance to be trumpeted in our secular world?

Is it not also a highly significant fact that, hitherto, all generations since the beginning of time have managed the intimacy of their married lives quite adequately without explicit sexual education, illustrated, to guide them?

---

[*] I most strongly recommend *Sex Instruction in the Home*. See Book List, page 162.

31

Sexual Morality

What is the right use of our sexual faculty? What would please our loving Creator? What is God's Will? It is essential to establish the chain of linked teaching in this emotional and contentious area of human conduct, where all of us experience great temptation throughout our lives, an area in which there must be an unceasing build-up of resistance. We can be cheerful because God's reward of happiness in His love will infinitely surpass all the denied pleasures of sinful, sexual self-indulgence.

We know why Almighty God made us. It is a natural and logical aspiration, then, for us to want children of our own whom we can love and who will love us. He has given us the power to procreate them, the unique faculty of our reproductive organs. Additionally, in His Wisdom, He has attached a pleasurable aspect to the exercise of the reproductive function and given us a sexual desire to ensure the future of the human race, for as long and in such numbers as He wishes to keep it in being on earth.

God has given us three rules which can be briefly stated. Our sexual organs are not to be used solely for pleasure, by oneself or with any other person, male or female. Second, they are only to be used within marriage, an indissoluble union sanctified by the Sacrament of Matrimony. Third, the act of sexual intercourse must be open to the transmission of life. These rules are absolutely clear and unequivocal; they have been the teaching of the Church since it was founded. Advances in biological science have required the addition of a fourth: conception should only take place as a result of sexual intercourse, some limited assistance being permitted to encourage fecundity.

At an early age we learn a number of absolutes for our own safety and protection, for example, keep away from fire; later, do not use drugs. If an activity, smoking for instance, can be labelled 'unthinkable' in one's mind, it is easier never to engage in it or to be persuaded to do so.

All sexual activity outside marriage, homosexual as well as heterosexual, is forbidden by Almighty God. It must be labelled 'unthinkable', not even to be considered, no ifs or buts. The sexual activity referred to is of course sexual intercourse – how babies are conceived – and only husbands and wives have sexual intercourse together. Children, including adolescents, do not find this difficult to accept, even before they know what it means other than its being the way to have children. Indeed, the element of mystery helps.

Inevitably, children will learn about 'sex', losing some of their innocence, and may well stray into it. In contrast to the wonder of sexual intercourse between husband and wife, such acts strike their consciences as abuses, let-downs, falls from grace, and they feel ashamed. Treated gently and with understanding at Confession, they can be got back on track before their will is weakened. Celibacy before marriage should be taught without quibble or hesitation as the norm, and where there is the will, it is easily accepted (see Chapter 33).

The value of childlike, trusting innocence is incalculable and should be protected as long as possible. Tragically, it is being deliberately destroyed in schools at an ever younger age by compulsory, explicit description of the mechanics of sex in all its aspects, natural, unnatural and self-abusive. Such exposés are called 'sex education', but they are really the work of the Devil. He sees it as a dismantling of one of the bastions against sexual licence, the destruction of innocence, as well as an arousal of children's curiosity, the commonest reason for embarking on sexual activity by young people. Parents must beware and act to protect their children.

31 SEXUAL MORALITY

Sadly, close and intimate friendships at all ages have become victims of such a focus on sexual activity. Too often an association between two people of the same or different genders, irrespective of age, is perceived as a 'relationship' with an actual or potential sexual content. Ordinary companionship is a victim: so many close friends of every age are widely regarded as not normal unless they are 'in a relationship'. Additionally, a man's friendship with a young boy or a young girl, which can be so enriching, risks being labelled an illegal 'relationship' with subsequent arrest and court action. Also, teachers have been exposed to accusations of sexual assault when they have only been showing needed friendly affection towards some of their pupils with family problems at home.

A 'relationship' is a euphemism for a sexual liaison between 'partners': a boy and a girl, a man and a woman, or between two people of the same gender. Some last for long periods; others are just brief affairs. All are intrinsically wrong.

The teaching of God is that either friendship or marriage – which gives rise to ties of kinship – are the only loving bonds: the former chaste and innocent, and the latter intimate when it has been blessed by the Church in the Sacrament of Matrimony.

Glance around at the consequences of disobeying God's rules of sexual conduct. Has casual fornication, undertaken by children as young as eleven or twelve, enriched the lives of young people? Has premarital sex made for happier marriages? Has divorce improved the lot of families and especially of children? Has the availability of contraception reduced the number of unwanted pregnancies or the number of abortions?

Most alarming of all has been the way scientists and doctors have invaded the human reproductive function. Questions are still being asked about the long-term effects on health of such serious interventions against nature as the pill, especially on teenage girls. In particular, what physiological and psychological damage is done to women who suffer the trauma of an abortion? Have these issues been honestly addressed? Will there be a parallel to the apparently deliberate blurring, to appease a vociferous pressure group, of the link between sodomy and Aids by unwarrantably including heterosexual intercourse as another common source of the disease instead of blaming promiscuous activity?

Even more serious has been the transfer of our generative function to the laboratory. There is artificial insemination including by donor, *in vitro* fertilisation, cryogenic embryo preservation for future use, trading ova and sperm in expensive medical procedures, intervention in genetic formulae, sexing human eggs like chickens, and treating so many innocent, embryo babies, dead and alive, with contempt. Millions of babies are slaughtered in the womb because they are unwanted or not up to a quality standard. Human cloning, alas, is inevitable. All this stems from an arrogant assertion that God has no part in procreation, and the denial that human beings have any future beyond life on earth. Scientists and doctors, plus politicians and lawyers, believe that they should control procreation, with or without parental approval, some parents reduced merely to being suppliers. Innumerable children will not know who their parents are and will be treated like pets. Where will it end? How long, I wonder, before an incubator is developed to replace a womb for breeding children without the need for a mother?

Many maintain that the Church has interpreted God's rules for sexual conduct too strictly, and that our freedom to enjoy a gift of God is more curtailed than it should be. What we really mean is 'than we want'! Is the Church not right, however, for once released from tight control, the demonic energy of sex driven by fantasy runs rampant? But for the firm teaching of the Church, Western society would sink into moral anarchy and the normal family unit disappear.

The linked chain then is this. We must serve God's purpose, not our own. He created us and keeps us in being. He has asked

31 SEXUAL MORALITY

us to do His Will. When we marry, it is to be an indissoluble union, for the sake of the man and the woman and that of any children. God will use a married couple to procreate children, or He may not. Any children issuing from the marriage, however, will be His gifts, the number of whose begetting we only have some ability to choose. That element of choice is a serious responsibility calling for periodic continence. The marriage act as an expression of conjugal love is a privilege as well as a pleasure. It is not an unrestrained right, neither to beget children nor to enage in solely for pleasure (CCC 2349; see also Chapter 32 para. 7). We may grumble and even chafe at this, but we cannot deny that it is the teaching of the Church, unchanged since its foundation by Jesus Christ.

At the end of the day, it is our Creator to Whom we shall answer for all our conduct on earth, where He has placed us so lovingly. It is His judgment, not our own, which will determine our eternal future. We shall wake up to God.

Heed, therefore, the teaching of His Son, Jesus Christ; our eternal happiness is at stake.

> Dear Lord and Father of mankind,
>   Forgive our foolish ways!
> Reclothe us in our rightful mind,
> In purer lives Thy service find,
>   In deeper reverence praise.
>
> In simple trust like theirs who heard,
>   Beside the Syrian sea,
> The gracious calling of the Lord,
> Let us, like them, without a word
>   Rise up and follow Thee.

O Sabbath rest by Galilee!
  O calm of hills above,
Where Jesus knelt to share with Thee
The silence of eternity,
  Interpreted by Love!
Drop Thy still dews of quietness,
  Till all our strivings cease:
Take from our souls the strain and stress,
And let our ordered lives confess
  The beauty of Thy peace.

Breathe through the heats of our desire
  Thy coolness and Thy balm:
Let sense be dumb, let flesh retire:
Speak through the earthquake, wind and fire,
  O still small voice of calm.

– What an inspiring prayer! Its full beauty and meaning and value are not realised when it is sung as a hymn, uplifting though that is, words and music complementing each other. Learn it, sing it, meditate upon it and thank the Holy Spirit for His gift to John Greenleaf Whittier (1807–92).

– Likewise I recommend four other hymns:

'Soul of my Saviour', ascribed to Pope John XXII (1249–1334)

'When I Survey the Wondrous Cross', Isaac Watts (1674–1748)

'Praise my Soul, the King of Heaven', Henry Francis Lyte, (1798–1847)

'Lead us, Heavenly Father, Lead us', James Edmeston, (1791–1847)

They are found in every hymn book.

32

Contraception

An article of our Faith is belief in the resurrection of the body (see the Apostles' Creed). The human body shares in the dignity of 'the image of God', and the human person is a being at once corporeal and spiritual, body and soul, truly one (CCC 362–5). We do not have the right to do with our bodies whatever we wish.

The creation of the soul by Almighty God is at the moment of conception, that moment from which new life develops into a child to be born of its mother. All the constituent physical parts and genes exist from the moment of a child's conception, and those who argue that a fertilised ovum is not a new person, body and soul, at the beginning of his or her life and growth, fly in the face of all empirical evidence. This includes embryo babies which are frozen, many of which will die or be destroyed as part of an implantation procedure. How God in His loving mercy will protect and honour those martyred souls, tiny hapless victims all, must wait until He reveals Himself in His Kingdom. How, too, will He judge the mothers who yielded their ova to be so treated, or men their sperm? In particular, how will He judge single women who have a child but deny it a loving father?

My body is a gift of God and I am bound not to abuse it or its functions, not to damage my virtue or integrity, nor that of my neighbour, and not to take my life (CCC 2284–91). Actions which improve or protect my body's function, which are therapeutic, are not only moral but blessed, life and health being precious gifts entrusted to me by God.

A condom does not improve or protect a bodily function but is designed specifically to thwart one. It may provide some protection from a sexually transmitted disease, but that end does not justify a means which thwarts the natural God-given faculty to transmit life. Clearly the principal reason for using a condom is to do just this, without forgoing the pleasure of concupiscence or lust.

'Lust', and I quote, 'is disordered desire for, or inordinate enjoyment of sexual, pleasure. Orgasmic sex is morally disordered when sought for itself, isolated from its procreative and unitive purposes' (CCC 2351). This is the teaching of the Church; it is clearly stated. Harsh it may well seem, but only if insufficient account is taken of the purpose of our unique, God-given, procreative faculty (refer back to Chapter 29).

It should come as no surprise, therefore, that all means of contraception, mechanical, botanical or chemical, whether they interfere with natural ovulation, the life or mobility of sperm or are abortifacient, are likewise intrinsically wrong. So, too, are the surgical procedures of vasectomy and sterilisation. There is no end which justifies the use of contraception as a means to it. This is and always has been the teaching of the Church. It is not subject to majority vote or to individual choice. Abstinence may be a trial, like any self-restraint for a good cause, but it is quite normal and can be achieved with understanding and God's grace. There are no 'fundamental options' (refer to *Veritatis Splendor*').

God is the creator of life and He has endowed us with our procreative faculty; not only are we bound to use it responsibly and without abuse, like all our other God-given faculties, but we are fully able to do so, especially with His grace. Moreover, in His wisdom God has so regulated a woman's reproductive cycle that just by timely, short abstinences can the spacing and number of children born to married couples be chosen naturally and reliably. **To argue that a couple are unable to exercise restraint from time to time is to deny that we have free will; it also ignores the fact that such**

32 CONTRACEPTION

restraint is frequently exercised for many reasons in addition to the proverbial headache. It is to deny, too, that what we should be doing is God's Will, as we pledge in the Lord's Prayer, and not what we would like to do.

God created the world and all its people. He creates every baby that is born. Is it conceivable that He would overpopulate the earth? (What is overpopulation? See Chapter 36.) He created man with free will, and man's will would not be free if it did not include 'I will not'.

Again, it should come as no surprise that none of the stated objectives for the use of contraceptives are being achieved: the number of unwanted pregnancies and abortions continues to increase; so does the population of the world; and the incidence of Aids does not diminish. Nor, I suggest, is the increasing number of divorces unrelated to the use of contraceptives. (Ask youself: what reasons can you think of to support such a theory?)

Finally, once the integrity of the marital act, namely its being open to its unique God-given purpose, is compromised, there is no end to the abuse of man's reproductive faculty for intentions which may be popularly judged good or desirable but are not in accordance with God's Will as revealed to His Church (see Chapter 29).

In summary, the prime purpose of contraception is to close the marital act to the transmission of life, or to abort life, to thwart the unique and prime purpose of sexual intercourse, the procreative faculty given to us by God, which should only be used responsibly in conjugal love as He wills it. Contraception permits 'making lust', not making love in its totality. Hence His Church teaches that contraception is intrinsically wrong and forbids it. That purely physical pleasure take the place of the true and higher meaning of the marital act is unthinkable and that is the end of it.

Does this mean that their marriage is not consummated when a husband and wife begin married life using contraception?

This is a fundamental, indeed crucial, question. Search for the answer.

The *'Memorare'*

'Remember, O most loving Virgin Mary, that it is a thing unheard of that anyone ever had recourse to thy protection, implored thy help, or sought thy mediation, and was left forsaken. Filled therefore with confidence in thy goodness, I fly to thee, O Mother, Virgin of virgins; to thee I come, before thee I stand, a sorrowful sinner.'

Here make a special request to Our Lady ...

'Despise not my words, O Mother of the Word, but graciously hear and grant my prayer. Amen.

'O Mary, conceived without sin, pray for me who has recourse to thee.

'St Joseph, most chaste spouse of Mary, who exercised self-denial in your love for God and for your wife, help me to do likewise.

'May the Holy Spirit teach us again that the only human achievements of value to us and to society, and which will be pleasing to God, our Creator, are achieved by the power of self-denial, with which He blessed us in abundance, and which He will strengthen with His grace by request.'

✠

Until 1930 all Protestant denominations had been united with the Catholic Church in condemning the use of contraception. 'The Anglican Lambeth Conference', said editor James Douglas of the London *Sunday Express*, 'has delivered a fatal blow to marriage, to motherhood, to fatherhood, to the family and to morality.' *New York Times*, 17 August 1930. How prophetic he was!

33

Virginity, Chastity and Celibacy

Virginity has a divine purpose and parents have a responsibility to ensure, at home and in their educational role, that every son and daughter is aware of what a great and valuable gift it is, not in isolation but in the context of God's love and compassion. Virginity is not something to be lost, got rid of or thrown away, as if it was a drawback or an embarrassing condition; it should be preserved with great pride. Virginity is a mark of, and a shield for, personal integrity. Virginity may be dedicated to God by a professed celibate or presented as a unique and priceless gift to the person one decides to marry. It adds immeasurably to the value of a marriage and will be a positive factor in ensuring a loving, happy, faithful lifelong union.

The state of virginity and the practice of chaste celibacy should be immensely precious to boys and girls, to unmarried men and women, and praised as a mark of integrity and self-respect. Sadly for the happiness of us all, they are far from being so regarded. On the contrary, a man or a woman who is a virgin is widely taunted about it, regarded as not grown-up, immature, frightened of real living, while celibacy is labelled not normal, stifling and not good for one's health and well-being. **Indeed, chastity in thought, word and deed is derided, the very opposite of that virtue's highest esteem in the sight of God and prized above all by so many martyrs especially young girls.**

Not only has 'sex' been detached from our reproductive function, to stand alone as an activity to be indulged in as opportunities offer, but also the pleasure of such activity has been grossly exaggerated since it became a commonplace subject for writers of every kind. In particular, bodily union in sexual intercourse has been glamorized as though it were invariably blissful, which it is not in reality, as any married woman and many husbands will confirm. On the contrary, it takes time and loving tenderness for a couple to achieve sexual pleasure; God in His infinite wisdom has endowed with a bonus the lifelong fidelity He has com-manded.

Bernard Shaw observed: 'There is less difference between one young woman and another young woman than the average young man thinks', but that is not how young men feed their imaginations. Thus is a predatory element in the human male encouraged by Satan; just for pleasure, men give in to sexual greed and gluttony, the ego dominant, the other party a sensual convenience. Girls and women have been bullied by feminists on grounds of sexual equality to yield themselves, often promiscuously, although it goes against their deepest and strongest instinct, their maternal nature, and their desire for lasting love, protection and security. Lust is widespread.

All forms of sexual activity outside of marriage, including masturbation and homosexual practices by men or women, all of them mortal sins, are mere carnal experiences which provide moments of stolen pleasure. They are centred on self, empty of feeling, unsatisfying and never rise above exhaustion, meaningless ends in themselves. Secretiveness, which covers shame, or, contrariwise, an openly defensive attitude on the part of those who engage in such activities, confirm their hollowness. Freedom from guilt – reassurance – is sought by great numbers, and loud are the proclamations that everyone should carry on sexually as they choose. The seeds of concupiscence are sown in young people; they grow into plants which poison their hosts.

Such conduct offends and troubles us but may not directly touch us. There is one area, however, which deeply upsets all

33 VIRGINITY, CHASTITY AND CELIBACY

Christian parents, and indeed many other parents. It is the non-chalance with which their sons and daughters enter sexual relationships with girlfriends or boyfriends, despite the teaching of the Church and the advice of their parents. What can we do about it?

We can do nothing without the help of Almighty God. We must pray that He will intervene as He did many times in the Old Testament, first sending prophets and leaders, inspirational holy men and women both religious and lay, to speak up, and then wreaking punishment on the wrongdoers. (Read again the story of the golden calf in Exodus 32:1–35, referred to in Chapter 30.) The evangelical counsels of chastity, poverty and obedience apply not only to priest and nun but also to the laity: being a lay person is a vocation too.

'St Agnes, St Augustine, St Joseph and St Elizabeth, Duchess of Thuringia, pray for me.'

✠

– Look up the lives of these saints to find out why I have chosen their intercession at this point. Butler's *Lives of the Saints* is frequently in public libraries.

– A Courageous Witness:

'Those of us who practise medicine must state unequivocally that chastity* arising from self-restraint never did anybody any harm, and that the control of the sexual instinct is both possible and indeed necessary to the full maturing of human personality.'

Dr Ambrose King, a Chief Adviser to the Ministry of Health, 1941 Annual Meeting of the British Medical Association at Sheffield.

---

* so called because it chastises lust and concupiscence to be controlled by sense and will; modesty is its custodian.

34

The Priesthood

Obviously there is a great need to discipline and sanctify our bodies, which share in the dignity of 'the image of God', a task to which we give insufficient attention. The way to sanctification as well as salvation lies in the one, Holy, Catholic and Apostolic Church, the Church of our Baptism. This Sacrament and the other six are administered by Her priests, men who answer a call by God to devote their entire lives to Him and are ordained as ministers of the Sacraments.

'In the ecclesial service of the ordained minister, it is Christ himself who is present to his Church as Head of his Body, Shepherd of His flock, High Priest of the redemptive sacrifice, Teacher of Truth' (CCC 1458). 'Through the ordained ministry, especially that of bishops and priests, the presence of Christ as Head of the Church is made visible in the community of believers' (CCC 1549). Do we always recognise the presence of Christ in his priests? Do we at the same time appreciate that they have our human weaknesses and that, more than most, they need our daily prayers?

Souls can be saved other than as baptised members of the one true Church, but it is more difficult and perilous a road. Let there be no doubting that – not that it will be easy going for the Faithful, but they do have the huge advantage offered by the Sacraments, especially Confession and Holy Communion. Hence we Catholics have a duty and mission to convert our neighbour. (Let us remind ourselves that our neighbour is every man and woman, without exception, whom God has created and keeps in being – see Chapter 22.) This is the common priesthood of the Faithful exercised by the unfolding of baptismal grace, and that of Confirmation – a life of Faith, hope and charity, a life according to the Spirit (CCC 1546–7). By prayer and persuasion

34 THE PRIESTHOOD

we must try to bring our neighbours into the Catholic Church. 'Go therefore and make disciples of all nations, baptising them in the name of the Father and of the Son and of the Holy Spirit, teaching them to observe all that I have commanded you, and behold, I am with you always, even to the consummation of the world' (Matthew 28:19-20).

✠

The Apostles, therefore, were instructed to go forth and teach every member of every nation to be a disciple, a teacher, a missionary. **With God's abundant grace, which we have to seek, each of us must be a disciple sharing in the priesthood of Christ and being His witness (CCC 1536 – 1600).**

Witnessing to Christ has never been easy. After all, we have been told we must be prepared to suffer for the sake of the Gospel. 'The Church has a special esteem for her martyrs,' wrote Cardinal Basil Hume OSB in 1994. (My contemporary at Ampleforth: he joined the monastery straight from school, became a Housemaster and was elected Abbot; he was chosen as ninth Archbishop of Westminster in 1976.) Pope John Paul II also underscored the value of martyrdom ('*Veritatis Splendor*'). We are called to lead heroic lives and can do so with God's grace. There is no escape from the cross each of us must carry if we are to reach His loving arms. Let every sign of the cross X you make remind you of this.

A prayer to be said after every Mass

'O Lord Jesus Christ who has chosen the Apostles and their successors, the bishops and priests of the Catholic Church, to preach the true Faith throughout the whole world, we earnestly beseech Thee to choose from among us, especially in our family and our parish, priests and religious, brothers and sisters, to fall in love with Thee and gladly dedicate and devote their entire lives to make Thee better known and loved. Amen.

A prayer for onself

'Choose me, too, as Thy disciple, as well as Thy loving follower, not only by the example of holding to Thy precepts, but also by explaining them to my neighbour and so making Thee better known and loved. Amen.'

✠

In this Chapter I referred again to Baptism. Remember that we are baptised with the Sign of the Cross. What does that mean and why is it used?

'In the last letter Jim ever had from home and which he kept until his death, his father, a country pastor, hoped that 'his dear James' would never forget that 'who gives way to temptation, in the very instant hazards his total depravity and everlasting ruin. Therefore resolve never, through any possible motives, to do anything which you believe to be wrong.'

Lord Jim, Joseph Conrad

At a baby's Baptism, Godparents take on the responsibility of inculcating in their Godchild such a Christian resolve and must reinforce it regularly (see Chapter 2).

A perfect short prayer:

'Graciously impart unto us, we beseech Thee, O Lord, the Spirit at all times to think and to do the things that are right: that we who cannot subsist without Thee, may be enabled to live, according to Thy will.'

(Collect, Eighth Sunday after Pentecost, in my Roman Missal.) Say it. Meditate on all that it means. Memorise it. Recall it each time you are tempted to sin. Also, when you see an offence against God, or hear of one, say it for the offender; he or she, created and loved by Him like you and me, is our neighbour.

The Family is Fundamental

'Honour thy father and thy mother' (Exodus 20:12) is the Fourth Commandment, a high priority.

Think of the Holy Family, Mary, Joseph and Jesus: it is our role model, needed more than ever today as Satan tries to destroy marriage and the family unit. Additionally, in Jesus' time, the family relationship was much more extended, not only to blood relatives but to friends and associates. Loving their immediate neighbour was both practised and practical.

As a guide to our conduct and moral thinking, we can ask ourselves what Mary and Joseph would have thought or done in a particular situation we might be facing. Let such an exercise provide a back-up to that teaching of the Church which we might be resisting, and let us ask for their help to avoid mortal sin.

God created Adam and then gave him Eve. Although they disobeyed Him and fell from grace, not the best example to us, they were the first family, the first parents – and teachers – of children. Throughout history the family has been the essential unit of every community, the foundation on which society has been built. Without the family unit, society disintegrates. So does law and order. Do we not see this all around us?

All children have a father and mother and need a stable home. They had no part in their being brought into the world: it was their father and mother who were responsible and who, together, have a corresponding duty, cost what it may, to love, rear and educate their children. Every child is owed nothing less.

Let it be stressed again that every child is a gift from God, to be welcomed unreservedly, cherished and loved. No woman, married or single, has the right to have a baby, naturally or by biological intervention, and the life of a child from the moment of its conception is sacred, no matter what its physical condition. Remember that it is God who made the handicapped child too; He loves it and will take care of it. He also rewards its parents with joy, as the father and mother of any handicapped child will tell us, and He will ease their burden of caring for it. Think, too, of what some severely handicapped children and adults have been able to achieve. Helen Keller and Christy Nolan are but two well-known examples: they brought out the best in, and enriched, all with whom they came into contact. They are vessels full of endless love for their family. Go and read about their lives.

The plight of millions of children today is one of neglect, emotional disturbance, separation from or absence of a parent, deprivation of love, dire poverty, abandonment, cruel suffering, disease and tragically short lives. This is largely the result of power struggles between warring factions in a score of countries. In the Western world, however, countless children are the victims of broken marriages, single parents, sexual permissiveness and sexual abuse. In parts of Latin America, homeless children in some cities are killed like vermin. In China, second children are compulsorily aborted and many newborn girls are put out to die in the cold or drowned. There can be no excuses for such suffering by so many children, and we must do everything we can to re-establish protection and loving parental care for all children.

From the moment of conception, children are struggling for their birthright in a world without God intent on material welfare and selfish gratification. They suffer, too, from abandonment or erosion of personal and parental responsibility. The State and local authority are instructive agents, binding oragnisations and individuals in a web of criminal legislation, often ill-cosidered and arrogant, policed by inspectors and heavy penalties. The reaction? People look to blame others and take them to court to seek large compensation payments. Both trends are detrimental to a healthy society of responsible, self-reliant individuals and parents; they give children bad example.

In a world where the family has never been under such unrelenting threat, particularly from the State, and in which there have been so many unhappy and suffering children, should the Fourth Commandment, perhaps, be changed to 'Father and mother, honour your child'?

The importance of the family unit is inestimable, and no amount of sacrifice and self-denial is too high a price to pay to keep it intact until death. If the price is not paid on earth, be sure that this will be taken into account at the Last Judgment.

Who better than our Blessed Mother to pray to for families everywhere, and to do so by saying the Rosary *en famille*?

The Joyful Mysteries
1. The Annunciation
2. The Visitation
3. The Nativity
4. The Presentation
5. The Finding in the Temple

The Five Sorrowful Mysteries
1. The Agony in the Garden
2. The Scourging at the Pillar
3. The Crowning with Thorns
4. The Carrying of the Cross
5. The Crucifixion

The Five Glorious Mysteries
1. The Resurrection
2. The Ascension
3. The Descent of the Holy Spirit
4. The Assumption
5. The Coronation of Our Lady

The Rosary used to be a common family prayer. See what the *Catechism of the Catholic Church* now has to say (CCC 2685).

☩

The cult of one- or two-child families is not what God intended (Genesis 1:28) and casts a blight on the lives of us all. The role of the family is diminished. Divorce is easier and more common. One child or two can be divisive. One or two are more likely to be spoilt or indulged, to become selfish and delinquent. Three or more children, however, learn to live together and set good social standards, bring each other up and emerge with stronger, more upright characters, bound together as loving, supportive siblings. The larger the family, the more valuable it is to society. (Think about that last statement: how is it true?)

Not the least, common to all countries of Western Europe, are the pension and care burdens of a greater number and longer life of retired people than productive workers to provide the necessary support.

God knew what He was about when He said that we should increase and multiply (Genesis 1:28). To please God we must have more genuine families and more children.

Finally, take note that the terms brother & sister, aunt & uncle, and even husband & wife, may soon disappear.

Rosarium Virginis Mariae, John Paul II, 16th October 2002
The Five Luminous Mysteries
1. The Baptism of Christ in the Jordan
2. The wedding feast at Cana
3. The Proclamation of the Kingdom
4. The Transfiguration
5. The institution of the Eucharist

36

Killing and Stealing

The nations of the West are rich, all the resources of the earth at their beck; the deprivations of poor countries elsewhere are a scandal. This contrast is glimpsed all too rarely on our television screens, usually only prior to an appeal for funds to relieve a catastrophic situation. Then it comes off the screen and is forgotten (refer back to Chapter 1).

Not all deprivations and misery can be blamed on natural disaster, war and the greedy exploitation of finite natural resources. Frequently poor countries are the victims of rich nations with their predatory demands, often backed by the provision of finance at profitable rates of interest, which not only ravage their natural resources and local industries but also saddle them with heavy long-term debt.

Eighty per cent of the world's resources are consumed by 20 per cent of its people. Only quite a small percentage of available, suitable land – between 5 and 10 per cent – is cultivated for food, and in Europe farmers are being paid not to raise crops.

(Did you know that the whole population of the world in 1993 would fit comfortably into the State of Texas? Or that with the same population density as London, only two Texases would accommodate ten billion people, double the present number?)

Meanwhile the fertility of poor women, especially in underdeveloped or heavily populated countries, is blamed for every problem, including shortage of food. Hence regular aid from the West has been linked to enforcement of artificial birth-control programmes, including abortion. This is bullying, offensive and often contrary to deeply held principles, especially in societies where people see children as valuable, productive additions to a family and the community. Moreover, empirical evidence does not support the argument that population growth adversely affects economic development; rather, the opposite applies.

Most of us have accepted what we have been told about the number of people on earth, that the world is overpopulated and numbers are still growing, particularly in China, India and parts of Africa, and that it cannot support such numbers. This is a subject which will repay serious study (refer back to the previous chapter). I believe there is no cause for gloom. After all, it is God who puts people in the world, keeping men and women in equal balance, and He does so out of love. Would He overpopulate the earth and create misery? Is it overpopulation, so easy to blame, or is it other human factors – i.e. our fault – which cause the problems in the so-called Third World? How often since Malthus has the doom forecast failed to materialise, and still the population of the world continues to grow?

(If a country's population does not grow, it can rapidly go into decline, in numbers and economically.)

Let us get back to the subject of the chapter. It is about the Fifth and Seventh Commandments – 'Thou shalt not kill' and 'Thou shalt not steal' (Exodus 21:13,15) – two rules for behaviour towards our neighbour. We know what the words say, but do we know what they cover? Coupling them – they both forbid taking something – will enable us to appreciate how much more they mean. Together they occupy eighteen pages in the *Catechism of the Catholic Church*, a lot more than most of us might imagine. They are often broken in their wider context, as indicated earlier.

They do have a clear bearing on the poor and needy in our own countries and on the deprivations of so many peoples throughout the world. Their plight is not to be addressed out of charity or largesse, but as bounden duty. We must think of the deprived, picture them often in our minds, as we live our comfortable lives. What shall we, who comparatively have in abundance, do to help them, to provide them with what they do not have? Do we, at the very least, remember them daily in our prayers?

It is fundamental that the only people who can really help the poor are the rich. Only those who 'have' can give to the 'have-nots'. Who gave the 'haves' what they possess, and the wealthy their money and riches? **Everything comes from God – and it is only on loan.** We shall be answerable to Him for our stewardship as members of a world community.

What about the sale of arms? Is there a limit to the money or possessions which one can properly keep? What is our responsibility for the environment? Think on these questions, not under one or other of the two Commandments but both coupled together.

The evil of abortion, which offends both of them, has already been referred to and will be dealt with in the next chapter. Of much greater significance to the old and the infirm, however, is how soon the reasons for control of life in the womb – over 50 million abortions a year – will be extended to cover their lives. Should those of us who have reached three score years and ten, the so-called allotted span, or younger people with an incurable disease or incapacity, fear for our futures because we do not measure up to standard, or are not wanted by relatives or by society? Or because we have become disproportionately expensive to keep? My answer is the prayer which follows, and into which I should have liked to insert something about a shield against euthanasia.

'O Lord, support us all the day long until the shadows lengthen and the evening comes and the busy world is hushed and the fever of life is over and our work is done. Then, Lord, in Thy mercy, grant us a safe lodging, a holy rest, and peace at the last. Amen.'

John Henry, Cardinal Newman 1801–90

Oxford scholar and theologian, Anglican leader of the Oxford Movement; became a convert; founder of the Oratory of St Philip Neri in Birmingham; created a Cardinal in 1879. Newman's cause for canonisation is being pursued as I write.

☩

The larger issues should not be allowed to displace completely the threat to private property. Theft, mugging, robbery, burglary, looting, kidnapping and piracy, undertaken by small children, teenagers, opportunist men and women and 'professionals' (*sic*), has become an epidemic, a disease in the community and the world at large.* Many reasons are given but they are all materialistic. In fact such crime is widespread and growing because the Seventh Commandment is not taught and enforced from an early age. Unless this is remedied, the scale of the stealing of private and public property, and the holding of people for ransom, will continue to increase. Moreover, the natural resources of our planet, mineral, vegetable and animal, will be looted to the point where the earth will not be able to sustain mankind.

Greed and gluttony are capital sins. They lead to killing and stealing. Society is being destroyed, as is the earth we inhabit. Self is put before all, take before give, envy and hate before love of neighbour.

Whatever man touches without reference to God's purpose for it he destroys. This will surely lead to his own destruction. Wake up to God!

---

* Had there been no shoplifting or in-store theft in Britain in 1995, retail profits would have been higher by no less than 21 per cent and shop prices *pro rata* lower.

Abortion

Do we know the four sins crying to Heaven for vengeance (CCD 327 and CCC 1867)? Look them up and ask yourself why they were singled out. One of them is the sin of Sodom, both an unnatural act and an abuse of man's reproductive faculty. There is a strong case for adding another: abortion, a sin against the Fifth Commandment.

Abortion is the destruction of an innocent, helpless baby in the womb of its mother, probably the most pernicious act in the world today. It is an excommunicable offence – *latae sententiae* – for all those who take part in the foul deed (CCC 2272).

As already stated, fifty million abortions are taking place in the world every year. Just imagine, if you can, the equivalent of almost the whole population of Great Britain cruelly killed as babies in the womb every twelve months. Nearly one million a week! Imagine, too, the tiny shrieks of pain – if only they could be heard – before the tiny infants, torn to shreds, die and are still! 'Lord, have mercy on those who are responsible. Have mercy, Lord, on us also, who allow it to happen, or have not found a way to halt the callous and cruel slaughter of so many innocent souls. Mary, our Mother, beg thy Son for our forgiveness.'

Selfish man takes the view that if a child in the womb, innocent and defenceless though it may be, the blameless result of a rape, for example, is not wanted or has a defect, then it is right in conscience to kill it. This is condemned by the Church, teaching reaffirmed by Pope John Paul II in his encyclical *'Evangelium Vitae'* ('Gospel of Life'), 1995. It is against the Hippocratic oath which used to be taken by the medical profession (for healing) that does the killing. It is against the general view everywhere that taking human life is wrong and evil. (There can be, however, exceptions to that last statement: see CCC 2259–67 and 2302–17.) Almost everywhere capital punishment is banned: the lives of those guilty of having taken a life are saved. The innocent little child, however, is cruelly murdered in the womb without a second thought. The killer? A doctor who is paid a fee for the 'termination'.

If the mothers concerned were aware of how the lives of their babies would be snatched, could watch their tiny faces as they struggled and died, or were to see the mutilated little bodies being put in the waste bin for conveyance to the incinerator in thousands every week, would the light of their consciences be lit again?

We have all read stories of mothers giving their lives to rescue their babies, of others putting their lives at risk for the safety of their children. We know that the great anxiety of a mother likely to lose her life when pregnant is whether her unborn baby will be saved; if it is a choice between the life of mother or baby, the mother will choose that her baby should live and hope that she too may be saved. That is her maternal instinct and it is very strong. How many mothers have been burnt to death or drowned trying to rescue their little ones? What damage then is done to her maternal instinct and her character when a mother consents to an abortion? Do not overlook, however, how much pressure such mothers are under – although this is no excuse – as victims of callous men, of society and of a medical profession that has surrendered its respect for innocent life in the womb.

The fathers of aborted babies are rarely mentioned. Whether they know of the abortion or not, when their child is killed in the womb they are guilty of breaking the Fifth Commandment and must suffer the consequences of such a grave sin. They may escape the searing pain of the pitiless destruction of their child, but not the responsibility for its procreation and then its abandonment.

37 ABORTION

Do you remember what Jesus in His anger did to the traders in the temple (Matthew 21:12)? What would He have done to a surgeon and his abortion team in the operating theatre of a hospital, an institution in which the sick and dying are tenderly nursed and cared for, and where other babies are brought safely into the world, many treated with loving, twenty-four-hour intensive care?

What are we doing to stop abortions? Or even to prevent just one killing of a child in the womb? If we do nothing else, we can at least pray each day that every mother will have the strength to change her mind at the last minute and bear her baby. Pray especially to the Blessed Virgin Mary, who probably herself experienced pressure to abort the child in her womb.

Psalm 12:1-5: a cry for help and a promise:
'Help, Lord, for there is no longer any that is godly; for the faithful have vanished from among the sons of men.
'Every one utters lies to his neighbour; with flattering lips and a double heart they speak.
'May the Lord cut off all flattering lips, the tongue that makes great boasts, those who say: "With our tongue we will prevail, our lips are with us: who is our master?"
'"Because the poor are despoiled, because the needy groan, I will now arise," says the Lord: "I will place him in the safety for which he longs."

To this end, **Holy Water**, used since the early days of the Church, **is a powerful and effective sacramental**, a means of spiritual wealth deserving an eminent place in every home. Pope Pius IX spoke of its sanctity, virtue and benefits, urging frequent and fervent use to purify and preserve the soul and body. Its devout use remits venial sins and temporal punishment due to sin, one's own and that of a soul in Purgatory; it can heal the sick; it averts spiritual and temporal dangers*. As you enter and leave home make the Sign of the Cross with Holy Water, for your family and friends, the Holy Souls and yourself. Your prayer will reach them instantly and be effective. **Also, always carry a small bottle of Holy Water with you.**

☫

Abortion is the greatest deliberate slaughter of mankind the world has ever seen. The killing is thirty times that of Auschwitz every year. Each time we take a breath, about every four beats of our heart, the hearts of five little babies in the womb are forcibly stopped by a doctor. Is there a more heinous act than abortion? Yet it has the approval of the law in almost every country on earth.

When an innocent life can be cruelly stolen quite legally, it is no wonder that murder is on the increase. Or that so many help themselves to money and property which does not belong to them. Be sure that the old and infirm will soon be at risk from euthanasia. Pray to God for His mercy on us all.

Finally, a state of affairs upon which to reflect: infanticide is universally condemned as murder, whatever the child's physical or mental condition, and yet a baby boy or girl only a few weeks younger, so often a baby in the best of health, can be killed quite legally almost everywhere in the world: this is when the child is killed by a qualified doctor invading the womb in which the baby is being nurtured by its mother, and it is called abortion.

Equally absurd, violence and lewd conduct in public lead to immediate arrest but both are explicitly shown in almost every TV soap, sitcom and play, and in the cinema. Can there be any surprise, therefore, that, off-screen, crime engulfs us? Or that, morally, a sense of wrong-doing is replaced by self-indulgent justification in consciences informed by a secular, materialistic, greedy society?

---

* Ask your parish priest to teach you about this wonderful gift of God and the indulgence to be gained by using Holy Water, which he can dispense.

38

Live in Truth

The Eighth Commandment is: 'Thou shalt not bear false witness against thy neighbour' (Exodus 20:16; Deuteronomy 5:20).

When asked to list the Ten Commandments, this is the one which many of us most frequently cannot remember. If we are honest, that is when the first two are also excluded! The First is a long one, difficult to remember; the Second is the one overlooked when we are annoyed and swear, uttering a profanity. (What does this word mean? How seldom, surprisingly, does one hear it used – or the word obscenity – to describe language increasingly heard!)

The Eighth Commandment enjoins us to live in the truth; hence we must search for it and then bear witness to it (CCC 2464–513). Respect for the truth by individuals; by those responsible for education, especially our moral upbringing and the welfare of our spirit; by the media which daily reaches into everyone's mind through the newspapers and television; by those, too, who entertain us and who stimulate our thinking, senses and feelings through the arts, literature, stage, screen and television; respect for the truth by all these is a responsibility that must not be underestimated. Failure to take into account the possible effect on an audience of how those in it will think, act and behave, an effect which may be unseen or, heedlessly, even unsuspected, will nevertheless be on the record at the Last Judgment of those responsible. This will be in addition to the long list of personal wrongdoing of which we have all been guilty, and for which we shall have to account.

In particular, politicians whose respect for the truth and principle has fallen dramatically – as a result of politics having become a well-paid career – will have to answer for their deceit and hypocrisy. Let me quote a letter in the *Daily Telegraph* (26: xi: 94) from Robert Wylie of Burton-in-Wirral, following the resignation of a senior Member of Parliament from a Conservative Party office after writing an article accurately describing two of Britain's partners in Europe: 'Is it not strange that the politician who speaks the truth is forced to apologise and resign? The ones who lie to us daily remain in the top jobs and rule over lives.' How well he made his point! Food for thought too.

'Inspire me, O Lord, with a holy aversion to falsehood and dissembling, to cunning and indiscretion. May I avoid in my own person the faults I cannot suffer in others! May I prefer an obscure and hidden life to a life that is attended with pomp and significance! May I seek less what might attract admiration, and more that which would render me better. May I commit, O my God, both Thy graces and favours, to the safeguard of humility; that, notwithstanding the temptations and combats of this life, I may find in the peace of my heart a foretaste of Eternal felicity. Amen.'

The Imitation of Christ Thomas à Kempis who was an Augustinian canon and religious writer in Germany. (1379-1471).

His *Imitatio Christi* has been translated into more languages than any other book except the Bible.

✠

Finally, the feasts of St Stephen, first martyr, and St John the Evangelist follow the Nativity; what is the Church telling us? Then the Feast of the Holy Innocents; pray for them and for the millions of babies now cruelly killed in the womb every year.

The Tenth Commandment

What is the Tenth Commandment? How does it differ from the Ninth? In fact it forbids two of the capital sins, avarice and envy. (Can you remember what PALEGAS stood for? It is in Chapter 18.) The *Catechism of the Catholic Church* refers to the first Beatitude (CCC 2556) in the section on this Commandment.

Since this is a DIY handbook, a primer, one of its aims is to urge readers to search for greater knowledge by research and study. That is why I have not quoted this Commandment. Look it up if you have forgotten it. There are also several pages in the *Catechism of the Catholic Church* that deal with it.

The Beatitudes from the Sermon on the Mount:
'Blessed are the poor in spirit, for theirs is the Kingdom of Heaven.
Blessed are those who mourn, for they shall be comforted.
Blessed are the meek, for they shall inherit the earth.
Blessed are those who hunger and thirst for righteousness, for they shall be satisfied.
Blessed are the merciful, for they shall obtain mercy.
Blessed are the poor in heart, for they shall see God.
Blessed are the peacemakers, for they shall be called sons of God.
Blessed are those who are persecuted for righteousness' sake, for theirs is the Kingdom of Heaven.

Blessed are you when men revile you and utter all kinds of evil against you falsely on My account. Rejoice and be glad, for your reward is great in Heaven.'
(Matthew 5:2–11 and CCC 2546)

– The Beatitudes take on a whole new meaning when it is clearly understood that they are not referring to others but to me – and to you, dear reader. For example, it is we who should be poor in spirit, and this means to be detached from riches. Or take the fourth: read it as 'Blessed are **you** who hunger and thirst for righteousness'; it means you who yearn, to be good or holy, for example, to achieve or seek righteousness.

– What do you think the second Beatitude really means?

– I wonder why – except in the last – Jesus did not say 'yours' or 'you' instead of 'theirs' or 'they'? I must ask Him.

– Vatican II stressed the importance of the Beatitudes to the laity in undertaking their mission. Since then, 'Blessed' has selectively been changed to 'Happy': ask yourself by whom? Why? And how has it altered the meaning?

✠

The underlying counsel of the Beatitudes is to urge humility. This is the contrary virtue to pride, the capital sin of overbearing self-assertion, an offence which can go as far as the denial of one's complete dependence on God. How often does this result in 'I will' instead of 'I won't', as a deliberate refusal to accept a particular teaching of the Church, often one which we have not researched at source or learnt thoroughly?

– Now, let me refer you back to the first two paragraphs of this chapter. Not studying and learning the doctrine of the Church is, in effect, resisting the known truth, a sin against the Holy Spirit. Is it not also being short-sighted and foolish?

40

Priorities

While the absence of economic justice at home and overseas needs to be tackled with determination and vigour, we must not forget Original Sin and the Fall of Man. Adam and Eve, prompted by Lucifer, chose to do what they wanted rather than what God had commanded, and so lost their supernatural life. Man has been defying God ever since the Fall and has suffered, and will continue to suffer, as a direct result, not only physically but also in material terms. Wicked men and women now roam widely, tempting us to moral decay. Disease and pain and death are our certain lot; so too, in our own country and scattered across the globe, are hardship and poverty and war.

What then does our Lord mean when He declared: 'Seek first His Kingdom and His righteousness, and all these things (food, drink and clothing) shall be yours as well' (Matthew 6:33)? Also, we remember His reference to 'the birds of the air' and 'the lilies of the field' (Matthew 6:26–7). In particular, let us recall Jesus' admonishment: 'O men of little faith! And do not seek what you are to eat and what you are to drink, nor be of anxious mind. For all the nations of the world seek these things: and your Father knows that you need them' (Luke 12:30).

His message is that our soul has priority over our body. So does the next life over our time on earth. We should be content with, and not worry about, our lot in this life. **In addition to the word of Jesus Christ, we have the example of so many of the saints and martyrs: they have devotedly endured poverty, hardship and suffering, mortified their bodies and offered up their lives to save their souls.** The Church teaches the importance of prayer, fasting, abstinence and penance. You and I can tend and heal our souls and prepare them for life everlasting – or condemn them – but the time we have in which to do this here on earth is entirely in God's hands. Since He loves us He wants us to succeed, He will give us all the nourishing, healing and sanctifying grace we ask Him for. It is entirely up to us. Therefore we offer Him our lives to be saved.

In short: 'I place my trust in my Creator and pray that I do His Will, take up my cross daily (Luke 9:23) and try to relieve my neighbour of the cross he or she bears.'

Unless we search for and determine God's Will and strive to do it, unless we give priority to saving our souls, we shall be easily misled or persuade ourselves that material need comes first. When we do this, however, we know that selfish desires readily turn into needs we feel we must meet. The evidence is all around us.

More generally, humanism and liberation theology cause us, through misplaced compassion, to ignore God or to put Him second, even to usurp Him. Protestantism, moral relativism and subjectiveness all involve attributing to God how we, collectively or individually, have interpreted His teaching, rather than holding to what He has revealed it to be through His Church. These 'isms' elevate conscience to the extent that 'my conscience is clear' is used to justify any desired belief or action. Look around at some of the results and think about how you might prevent them.

'Most Sacred Heart of Jesus, through the intercession of Thy faithful servants, have pity on the poor people who do not know Thee, or who suffer severe hardship. Bring them to Thee and save them. Give to all priests, brothers and sisters and especially to lay men and women, strength to carry on in Thy service. In particular, grant perseverance to all aspirants to the

40 PRIORITIES

religious life and the grace of vocations to the priesthood to many young men. **Give me the grace and privilege to take my share in spreading Thy Word and doing good works throughout the world. Amen.'**

✠

Let me give you a useful guide to the priorities of charity, the love of one's neighbour:

The Seven Spiritual Works of Mercy:
1. To convert the sinner
2. To instruct the ignorant
3. To counsel the doubtful
4. To comfort the sorrowful
5. To bear wrongs patiently
6. To forgive injuries
7. To pray for the living and the dead

The Seven Corporal Works of Mercy:
1. To feed the hungry
2. To give drink to the thirsty
3. To clothe the naked
4. To harbour the harbourless
5. To visit the sick
6. To visit the imprisoned
7. To bury the dead

– Not to share with others what we have been blessed with, both spiritually and corporally, is an injustice.

Finally, think about this:

First man: "Sometimes I would like to ask God why He allows poverty, famine and injustice to continue when He could do something about it."

Second man: "What is stopping you?"

First man: "I am afraid He may ask me the same question."

41

Conscience

God has built laws into our soul as well as our body. Just as defiance of the laws which govern our physiology cause us pain, malfunction and even death, so by like defiance can we also damage our soul and even cause its death to God. In the soul, pain is an awareness of evil, a reminder of what we ought to do, of what is right and wrong. We have all felt the painful pricking of conscience. We all know, however, that conscience – for this is our guardian against wrong – can be distorted by the intellect, that popular argument can sway one's opinion, numb the conscience, banish guilt and shame.

Obviously, conscience must first be formed, that is, informed of the true teaching of the Church, taught what man is for, his complete dependence on God, what is right and wrong and how he can achieve his end. Only then can conscience serve its purpose of protecting an immortal soul from evil. Reason and will are the soul's gatekeepers, and the most effective of these is will.

It is worth quoting the Scottish Bishops on '*Humanae Vitae*' and Conscience:

'An issue that has been raised in connection with the Encyclical is the place of conscience. Man has the right and duty to follow his conscience. This is certainly true, if it is properly understood. Man is not a law unto himself; his conscience is not completely independent. The role of conscience is indeed to judge whether our actions are good or bad. But these judgments must be based on sound principles of right or wrong. The second

41 CONSCIENCE

Vatican Council in its declaration on Religious Freedom had this to say: "In forming their consciences, Christians must pay careful attention to the holy and certain teaching of the Church. For by Christ's Will the Catholic Church is the keeper of truth: it is her task to declare and teach authentically the truth which is Christ. She also has to use her authority to expound and support the principles of the moral order which have their origin in the actual nature of man."

(Part of the Scottish Episcopate's Pastoral Letter in 1968)

'Man is endlessly ingenious in discovering ways of misusing his reason. The commonest way is to leave it unused or to bypass its use ... He thinks with reluctance, which makes him a slave to habit. He thinks with the will, which makes him a slave to desire. He thinks with the imagination, which makes him a slave to slogans. Not using the full power of his mind, he loses perspective. Things closest – that is, close to the body's power to respond to them – loom biggest ... Man is intensely gullible: offer him what he wants to hear and you have him.'

Society and Sanity, F. J. Sheed

Once properly formed, conscience must be kept sharp and be heeded. In particular, it must be protected from: (a) turning a blind eye; (b) compassionate judgment; (c) numbing familiarity; and (d) popular opinion or fashion. To prompt a resolve by my reader to sharpen his or her conscience – as I must hone mine – ponder awhile on what those four terms mean in effect.

Here are my interpretations:

(a) 'What they do is not my concern.'

(b) 'The baby would have been significantly deformed and so it was aborted.'

(c) 'That was not soft porn but a description of bad behaviour essential to the plot of the story.'

137

(d) 'Everybody does it now.'

Let these prime further study to sharpen your conscience so that it will always be able to tell you clearly whether or not a passing or a planned thought, word or deed would be pleasing to God.

At the end of our days on earth, it is how closely we followed God's Word, and hence the extent of our love for Him, which will be judged and which will determine our eternal future.

The Church's teaching on 'Moral Conscience' is summarised in brief in the *Catechism of the Catholic Church* (CCC 1795–1802). We all need refreshers on this subject.

'To lose my life for Christ is to give myself up entirely to Him; to give myself up to Him is to love Him, and love is of the will. Our age is one of sentimentality, even to spiritual things. To live by faith and to seek only the Will of God is the way to peace, courage and happiness. Dispose of me, dear God, according to Thy will. Amen.'

A prayer adapted from one said by Cardinal Merry del Val, of precious memory.

✠

In a radio broadcast at Rochester, NY, on 16 June 1941, Sir Winston Churchill (1874–1965) said: 'The destiny of mankind is not decided by material computation. When great causes are on the move in the world ... we learn that we are spirits, not animals, and that something is going on in space and time which, whether we like it or not, spells duty.' Was not the great man speaking of conscience?

42

Grow in Study

To ensure that we do not stray on our journey to salvation, a pilgrimage demanding discipline, self-denial and, yes, suffering, the carrying of the cross laid upon each of us as a result of Original Sin, we must know what is the path of truth and study it in detail.

It is interesting to note that the one virtue which Jesus was described as having learnt was obedience. 'Although He was a Son, He learnt obedience through what He suffered; and being made perfect He became the source of eternal salvation to all who obey Him' (Hebrews 5:8–9). Also: 'He humbled Himself and became obedient unto death' (Philippians 2:8). He signposted the path and He gave us a supreme example to follow. We shall have no excuse if we do not obey the Commandments He asked us to keep, and so forfeit His love. **'If you keep My commandments, you will abide in My love, just as I have kept my Father's commandments and abide in His love' (John 15:10).** We need to learn humble obedience, as He did.

Vatican Council II reaffirmed all the doctrines of the Faith and the Mystical Body of Christ. The Faithful, baptised members of the Church, were enjoined to follow Her teaching and to believe in Her infallibility. In particular, Catholics must practise what they are taught by the Church and be witnesses of Christ to all non-Catholics.

The Council laid stress on the need of the Faithful to read the Bible, both the Old and the New Testaments, and for the bishops and priests to preach on biblical texts. Thus at every Sunday Mass we now have two readings of the Scriptures and one from a Gospel;

also a homily from the celebrant to explain them and to develop our knowledge of what the Church teaches.

Have we been obedient to Vatican II, after having read at least some of its documents, by reading the Bible and studying the teaching of our Holy Mother the Church?

Only members of the one, Holy, Catholic and Apostolic Church are sure of salvation (can we now explain why?), but only provided that we go to our Judgment in a state of grace. This means that we must have done our utmost to do God's Will, and be truly repentant of all our trespasses against Him. If we are not saved, it will be our disobedience and defiance which will have condemned us to eternal separation from the happiness of the love of our Divine Creator.

Indeed, if we do not save our souls, it will unquestionably be our own fault, and a lack of adequate study will have contributed. Life is a *status via*, a journey to God on which there is no stopping and no turning back. It is a journey full of pitfalls and buffetings designed by the Devil to trip us; he will also show us seductive side-tracks down which we turn at our peril. Throughout our journey, however, God has lit the right path and provided a secure chain handrail. Moreover, at every step of the way there is always His helping hand if we reach out and ask Him for it.

Before we set off on an unknown journey to any important destination, do we not make sure we have all we need to get there, carefully study the route and be prepared to ask for help if we stray? There is no journey more important than our life on earth, the final stage of which is taken at a time and place we never know beforehand. Be prepared!

'Our Lady of Fatima, Queen of the Holy Rosary, pray for us.'
Our Lady also taught the children at Fatima to say:

'O my Jesus, pardon our sins: save us from the fire of Hell and deliver the souls in Purgatory, especially the most abandoned.'

– Do you know the story of Our Lady of Fatima, the miraculous appearances by Mary, the Mother of God, and the simple message she gave to the world? (See the Book List: page 161.) Our Lady promises so much if only we do the little she asks. The fall of the Communist dictatorship in Soviet Russia was just one example of what she promised. The Mother of God is our mother, too, and like any mother she will not forsake us during our lifetime.

– I should like to add another prayer, the Collect from a traditional Mass for pilgrims or travellers:

'Be attentive, O Lord, to our entreaties, and govern the path of Thy servants and save Thou them, so that amid all the changes of our world and way, we may ever be protected by Thine aid. Through Jesus Christ our Lord. Amen.'

✠

'In those matters which pertain to faith and good morals ... as Augustine says in *De Doctrina Christiana* III: "Everyone should consult the rule of faith which he gets from the clearer texts in the Scriptures and from the authority of the Church." Therefore no one who assents to the opinion of any teacher in opposition to the manifest testament of Scripture or in opposition to what is officially held in accordance with the authority of the Church can be excused from the advice of being in error.' *Quaestiones Quadliberales,* St Thomas Aquinas *(Doctor Angelicus* and Confessor).

Pope John Paul II was much disliked by those who would like him to be more with it, up to date. In the sense that we all recognise an ultimate arbiter on moral questions, everyone has a pope; if it is not the real Pope, shall we not do what we want and believe only what suits us?

43

Grow in Prayer and Love

Not only do we need to learn about Christ and what He teaches, but also we need to know Him. This we only achieve in prayer. Prayer is not just something recited or read to Jesus, or thoughts or resolutions addressed to Him, although all may contribute. Especially it is the personal contact and spontaneous conversation which we have with a close friend.

God, our Creator, Who made us in His own image and alone sustains our life on earth; Who made us all that we are and has given us all that we have; He, our God, wants us to know Him, to love Him and to be happy with Him for ever. How valuable He has made us! Think about that. Pray about it. Learn to love Him.

His Son, Jesus Christ, has given us a promise: 'Therefore I tell you, whatever you ask in prayer, believe that you have received it, and it will be yours' (Mark 11:24). Does that not urge you to talk to Him? Above all, to listen to and learn from Him? To tell Him your thoughts and troubles? To ask for His advice and help? To place yourself in His love and keeping? That is what praying is : mental prayer, powerful and effective prayer rooted in love.

Suppose that someone to whom you had only been briefly introduced had then given you such a promise and ended with 'Give me a call'...

Jesus went on to say: 'And whenever you stand praying, forgive, if you have anything against anyone; so that your Father also, who is in Heaven, may forgive you your trespasses' (Mark 11:25). One could spend much time meditating on that advice.

In every chapter of this book I have provided a prayer. My idea is to encourage pause for thought as well as an opportunity to pray.

Some prayers will be familiar, others new to you; I hope you like them, that you will return to them and, therefore, to the tenets of the Faith sandwiched between them. Also, I hope readers will keep referring to the Book List for further reading and study.

Take on board a last meaning of the word 'primer': a primer is something used to trigger an explosive for detonation. (Can you remember the other three in the Preface?) With God's grace, I have been triggered – as I hope every reader will be – for an explosion, however small, of prayer and study, witness and good works. Writing it has also resulted in my seeking and buying a number of books, some for study, others for interest, all of which I have found absorbing and useful. They have been included in the Book List.

To finish this chapter, here is a reading from one of the Gospels. For over sixteen hundred years before Vatican II it was read at the end of every Mass, and it remains part of the traditional Latin Mass. It proclaims the divinity of the Incarnate Word, something too many of us have forgotten or deliberately ignore as we tend to please ourselves, and as we pick and choose from His teaching. No one should ever tire of reading and meditating upon it. Called 'The Last Gospel', it is the first fourteen verses taken from the Gospel written by John, the Beloved Disciple to whom Jesus entrusted His Holy Mother at the foot of the Cross.

'In the beginning was the Word, and the Word was with God, and the Word was God. The same was in the beginning with God. All things were made by Him, and without Him was made nothing that was made; in Him was life, and the life was the light of men, and the light shineth in the darkness, and the darkness did not comprehend it. There was a man sent from God, whose name was John. This man came for a witness, to give testimony of the light, that all might believe through him. He was not the light, but He was to give testimony of the light. That was the true light, which enlighteneth every man, that cometh into the world. He was in the world, and the world was made by Him, and the world knew Him not. He came unto His own, and His own received Him not. But as many as received Him, He gave them power to become sons of God, to those who believe in His name, who are born not of blood, nor of the will of the flesh, nor of the will of man, but of God, **and the Word was made flesh** [at Mass the standing congregation genuflect here] and dwelt among us: and we saw His glory as it were of the only-begotten of the Father, full of grace and truth.'

℟ 'Thanks be to God.'

St John the Evangelist

☩

Finally, some words of wisdom:

'Many things go to the making of man, but essentially it is the training of three aspects: body, mind and character. And neither mind nor character can be made without a spiritual element. That is just the element which has grown weak, where it has not perished, in our education, and therefore in our civilisation, with disastrous results. Nothing can be done till that element is restored.'

Sir Richard Livingstone, 1880-1960, classical scholar and educational reformer.

Please refer back to the three readings on page 10; what do Livingstone and à Kempis have in common?

Sixth edition postscript

Since 1996, scores of readers have kindly written to say that the value and benefit of my book grows every time they open it. They refer to it again, and again, and again. It has found a place on many a bedside table. *Gloria Spiritui Sancto!*

44

Trompe-l'oeil*

Viewed by a man or woman on the ground, the earth we inhabit looks flat. Seen from a great distance by an astronaut it is a globe, as it was made.

There are more than five billion people scattered all over the earth. Many of them are striving to lead 'good' lives, mindful that they are members of a community; others lie and cheat, rob and assault their fellows in advancing their own selfish interests; yet others are cruel despots who bully, torture and kill to establish their own fiefdoms of power.

While there is much that is good, generous, ordered, sadly there is also so much that is evil, selfish, disordered; many people are content but great suffering is being endured, not only as a result of deprivation, disease and disaster, but also by many who are clearly innocent victims of the behaviour of others.

How can such suffering be explained? How is the behaviour of evil people to be viewed? How do we assess our own? How should conduct be judged? By what criteria? Good or bad, harmful or harmless, of private or public concern, legal or illegal, right or wrong? In human terms only, each of us seeing it from an individual viewpoint? In what human terms? Is any assessment subject to the common rule of a higher authority? Should it be?

A conflict of views and consequent discordance must result unless there is an objective eye, a global viewpoint, providing an absolute definition and true perspective.

If we did not agree on a common meaning of the words used, we should be unable to communicate with each other. Is it not

---

* *Trompe-l'oeil;* drawing or painting designed to give an illusion of reality; make-believe (French: literally 'deceives the eye').

essential, likewise, to know something of metaphysics, the branch of philosophy dealing with the nature of existence, truth and knowledge? In fact, can we do without agreed, definitive answers to fundamental questions if we are to make sense of life on earth?

What is the purpose of the world and why are we human beings on it? Where did we come from? Are we free to do what we want here? How to explain suffering? Or the existence of evil? What comes after death? In short, what is my value? What meaning does life have?

We may see ourselves as we are, members of a family, relatives, friends, fellow citizens, overseas visitors and foreigners on an earth that appears flat. In fact we are all the same creatures of God and have transient lives here on earth. We are not autonomous, and owe all we are and possess to Him.

It is how our Creator sees us which is the true picture. Unless we strive to see why He made us, we shall have a distorted view of ourselves and the world we inhabit and never realise our true, eternal value to Him.

The enemy is liberalism in its religious sense. In Cardinal Newman's words, this is 'the doctrine that there is no positive truth in religion, but that one creed is as good as another... religion is not a truth but a sentiment and a taste; not an objective fact, not miraculous, and it is the right of each individual to make it say just what strikes his fancy'. In a secular world the reality of truth is denied; make-believe is the order of the day.

In contrast the most illiberal movement in the world is Islam, a psalm of which I shall now quote:

In the name of Allah, the All-merciful, the All-compassionate Allah, carry us in the ships of Your deliverance, give us to enjoy the pleasure of whispered prayer to You, make us drink at the pools of Your love, let us taste the sweetness of Your affection and nearness, allow us to struggle in You, preoccupy us with obeying You, and purify our intentions in devoting works to You, for we exist through You, and we have no one to meditate with You but You.

A Psalm of Islam

44 TROMPE-L'OEIL

- This prayer to Allah (God) could be said by Christians but I am using it as an opportunity to tell you about Islam.
- Islam was invented by Mohammed Ibn Abdullah (AD 570-632), an Arab born in Mecca, orphaned as a boy, a pagan, a camel driver, who gained respectability and influence by an early marriage to an older woman. Disillusioned by his affluent way of life, after a period of reflection and study, particularly of the Bible, he declared himself a prophet, law-giver and leader of his people, electing himself the Messiah, and writing the Koran, in which the New Testament was ignored and the divinity of Jesus Christ denied.
- Islam is a system of religion based on untruths, deceit and blasphemy initially spread by force of arms, illiberal and aimed at world supremacy, its followers almost successful in twice invading Europe, where now there is a huge number of Muslim migrants, as indeed in countries elsewhere in the world, making Muslims more numerous than Catholics. They have a higher birth rate; some 70 million hope to become citizens of the European Union; note, too, the worldwide proliferation of new mosques.
- Leanings of conversion from Islam are aggressively dealt with, and fundamentalist Islam is rigidly opposed to infidel Christianity, Holy Scripture and the Gospels and Judaism, Holy Scripture and the Gospels.

✠

Remember the key to Heaven is cut in the shape of a large cross; also that illusions of reality have a gripping appeal in a secular world. Life on earth can never be a bed of roses with all the thorns removed, as promised by the politicians, by medical research, by health & safety, by consumerism, by sex education and by peddlers of drugs. Christ suffered and died for us that we might be saved from sin, not from poverty, starvation and disease. His promise, as made to a sinner who believed and repented, is the only word on which we can utterly rely.

45
Personal Freedom

The Psalm of Islam, and so much else quoted in this book, calls for selfless dedication, sacrifice and self-denial. Where then is our freedom? What is personal freedom in a community?

The first thing to recognise is that personal freedom is always limited. There is no such thing as complete personal freedom: it is subject both to constraint and self-restraint, because one personal freedom inevitably encounters that of another person, thereby reducing both. Too much personal freedom, or too little, will progressively reduce it to the point where a few dominate and control the masses, who will then scarcely have any freedom at all. Obviously it is not easy to arrive at the right amount of personal freedom for a contented people. This also applies to my own conduct and my own contentedness. **Freedom, then, is the right to do only whatever we ought. It may not be easy to grasp at first but be sure that, paradoxically, the greater the self-control, the greater the freedom.**

This is not the way of the world. Increasingly secular with no belief in God or a hereafter, people are doing what they want and, increasingly, what they can get away with. They are their own judges; morality, especially with regard to sexual conduct, is now debatable. As a result, the political agenda has become paramount: the might of the State and local authority powers are entering more and more into the lives of people with a flood of legislation, regulation, exhortation and propaganda. The unelected bureaucracy in Brussels is an additional source of costly, regulatory legislation and it overrides our independence. 60% of our legislation is now dictated to us. No aspect of our way of living is immune, and interference and control become daily more intrusive and intimate.

All are prefaced with the intention of improving the lot of the people: their health, living conditions, education, working practices, environment, movement and leisure and, more recently, defence against terrorism.

This is at the expense of personal responsibility for oneself and one's dependents. The standards are set by government departments, special committees, bodies of experts and increasingly and more menacingly by self-appointed, lobbying single-issue groups. These activities soon become a political exercise where votes come before the welfare of the electorate. **In practice politicians can do little to improve but can easily worsen the welfare of the people.** Their policy is to placate those groups who shout most loudly, making promises, many of which will later be buried, to please the most people and win their votes. Sentiment glossily presented, a deliberate disregard of harsh truth, and scorn, rather than sound argument, win political power.

Two conclusions are quite clear: both the value and the destiny of man are ignored, and his freedom and responsibility seriously eroded. We are becoming enslaved, 'for your own good!'; 'in your own interest!' – like battery hens – soon to be legally put down at the end of our useful life. Morality is discarded and the concept of real well-being, the health of the spirit, has sunk without trace, a victim of the political pursuit of the 'feel-good' factor. (See Sir Richard Livingstone on page 144).

'God grant me the serenity to accept the things I cannot change, courage to change the things I can and the wisdom to know the difference.'

St Martin de Porres

– In an increasingly amoral world, this well-known and popular prayer may pose a risk of culpable complacency. In a secular society conduct is dictated by self-centredness and fashion: where it is evil it must be recognised and exposed, not passively accepted (Refer back to Chapters 18, 24 and 41).

☦

Guard against a peril of freedom!
Although the public has obtained food and drug regulations to protect physical and mental health, its demand that there be like restrictions in order to protect minds and characters from bad language, violence and sex in what we read, hear and see, is obstinately resisted. This is on the grounds of freedom of expression and the claim that the material objected to will have no decisive influence and so not cause any harm. The fact that millions are spent on advertising on screen and in the press because what we read, see and hear does influence our behaviour is conveniently ignored. The Devil aims to curtail freedom in a web of sin but here, instead, brandishing censorship as an enemy of freedom, he has imperceptibly enmeshed us.

If we reflect conscientiously on our viewing and reading, it will be apparent how much evil we have come to tolerate or ignore without demur. Further, what action are we taking to shield ourselves, our children and our neighbours from evil?

You may choose to refer back to Chapters 17 and 30 before continuing. I have deliberately used the word 'choose'. I want to emphasise that every action we take involves a choice. This is the one freedom of which we can never be deprived. **Remember, too, that it is according to how we have exercised that choice, our free will, that we shall be judged on the day we die.** This will include what we have chosen to tolerate or to ignore.

46

The Journey of Life

Human life is a journey between conception and death. **Like everyone on this earth, I was a microscopic creation by a loving God in the womb of my mother, all of me in being from the very instant of conception, and I am proceeding to the day my soul leaves my body, which will then crumble to dust.** Like everything in nature, a human body is governed by physical laws which keep it alive, those for breathing and blood circulation, for example, and over which we have little control; in particular we know not how long we shall live, when our heart might just stop beating for whatever reason.

We can, however, control our behaviour, how we think and act. Unless we adopt rules to govern and even limit our conduct, our freedom will diminish and could disappear. Moreover, the rules by which we live must be similar for all if order and harmony are not to be put at risk, if we are to avoid battles against each other as nations, tribes, and families – and even within families.

A human race living in harmony with nature and individually with each other was certainly the intention of our Creator, but God's dominion was defied (Chapter 2). Hence the history of the world and the deaths of so many of its inhabitants by violent means, fighting for autonomy and conquest. Hence the present disordered world and the plight, better or worse in our mortal state, of each one of us in it. Adam and Eve exercised their free will to do what they wanted and their descendants have been doing the same ever since.

How then should we choose our conduct?

Control of conduct may be of two kinds: imposed or voluntary. Natural law is imposed on all creation, which includes our bodies.

However, since men and women have free will, we can do or not do what we wish, subject only to physical limitations and the reaction of our fellows in the community in which we live. The rules of society, therefore, must be voluntary, self-imposed, respected and enforced; they take the form of civil and criminal laws introduced in a democracy by elected representatives. Otherwise there is disorder, or even anarchy.

Recall that everyone on earth was created by God and that He sustains each of us every moment of our being: all we are and have comes from Him. It is fundamental, therefore, that authority is from God, and that everyone in authority should serve Him. Those wielding authority may have inherited it, been elected to it or seized it, but it comes from God.

Natural law is integral, self-monitoring: it is a whole, linked inseparably from beginning to end. A general order, harmony and predictability are the result. It is marvellous to behold and a wonder of wonders. Nature's only enemy is man and his shortsighted, heedless exploitation of our natural resources always ends in their exhaustion and frequently in local human tragedies.

The laws of human society, on the other hand, are piecemeal: there are empty gaps between them and they vary significantly from one community, society or country to another, and by the efficiency of their enforcement.

In order to achieve a perfect world, is there any way that an ideal set of rules can be drawn up, that will be obeyed by everyone? Politicians and humanists try to persuade us so, but a glance around our local environment and the behaviour within it, more importantly a look into our own minds and hearts, will immediately convince us that Utopia can never be established here because we cannot agree on what we want.

Incidentally, the word 'Utopia' comes from the Greek: 'ou', not, and 'topos', place. Literally it means 'nowhere'!

46 THE JOURNEY OF LIFE

Back for the last time to the purpose of my book: protective help and a sure guide to the journey of life. Back, too, to the Garden of Eden, the birthplace of the human race and from which it was ejected as a direct result of its defiance of Almighty God, so making us all sinners.

Picture that in your mind once more to remind you of the calamity of the Fall, the victory Adam and Eve handed Satan.

Now recall the story of the good thief on Calvary: 'Truly, I say to you, today you will be with Me in Paradise.' All this sinner did was to proclaim his belief and pray: 'Jesus, remember me when Thou comest into Thy kingdom' (Luke 23:39–43).

Each one of us is even more fortunate than the good thief, for we have our Saviour's guarantee without asking for it. Redeemed on the Cross by Jesus Christ, we have His Church. He promised it would never founder, that no evil would prevail against it, despite 'the wickedness and snares of the Devil ... and all wicked spirits who wander through the world for the ruin of souls'. (From 'Holy Michael Archangel'; see Chapters 6 and 17. Have you memorised that prayer?) Christ's teaching, which is that of His one, Holy, Catholic and Apostolic Church, is infallible. It is a link chain the length of our journey which we must search for and tightly cling to the whole way, if we are to enjoy the love of God for all eternity. Our place with Him for ever is guaranteed if we hold on with one hand, keeping the other free to help neighbours journeying with us.

The chain is firm and inelastic, for there can be no compromise with truth. **Acceptance of truth requires the surrender of self – and of our sentiment – to the Will of God. Who He is, and what His Will is have been revealed to His Church and She teaches us unerringly, inspired by the Holy Spirit. Her teachings are the links in the chain and they are all in the *Catechism of the Catholic Church* (CCC), relevantly quoted throughout this book. We dissent from them at our peril.**

We must yield ourselves also in prayer, especially to Our Lady, Mother of Jesus and our Mother too, humbly to ask for the grace of our Almighty Father. He will surely grant us all we need to hold firmly to the chain, to overcome evil on the way and to step safely into His loving arms.

It is better to deny myself and to lose the whole world than to suffer the loss of my destiny with God in Heaven. Each of us must sacrifice self and suffer as Christ did to redeem us. What an example to follow! He was perfect and yet He surrendered Himself completely. We are imperfect, but with His grace we can follow His Word to resurrection in Him.

Denial of His love will result in failure to save my soul, a fate which is too awful to contemplate (see Chapter 24). Setting my will, what I think is right or what I desire – how often the latter determines the former! – against the Will of God; accepting the ever more hedonistic way of a secular world; putting man in God's place; loving me instead of Him; these will surely condemn my soul to eternal separation from the ever-loving God Who made me to be happy with Him for ever.

Me, who I am and what I do, held in being and enabled only by God, my Creator; me, I am but a few specks of dust compared to what I shall be and will enjoy if I yield myself to His Love, His Will, His Command, and so enter His Kingdom. Have not those who have yielded themselves, each in his or her own way, not been the happiest men and women on earth? Read the lives of the saints and martyrs.

Our whole life is but a fleeting moment compared to eternity (refer back to Chapter 13). A desire satisfied on earth is only a spark compared to the incandescence of God's love.

To render unthinkable a failure to achieve salvation and union with God, remember the four 'r's: read, reflect, react, repose. With questions to ponder, doctrine to research and study, this book is deliberately challenging. There are passages from Scripture to meditate upon and prayers to say, some of these carrying indulgences for the Holy Souls in Purgatory who will in turn pray powerfully for us.

In the Preface, I likened the teaching of the Church to a seamless knitted cloak, to protect and keep my soul until that happiest of days when God calls me to Him. Does yours, like mine, have holes to fill or repair?

Let us resolve, therefore, to develop our knowledge of God and His teaching through His one, Holy, Catholic and Apostolic Church by daily study and prayer, and to follow it. The reward for such discipline and self-denial when we come to yield up our life and its cross is guaranteed and will surpass all expectation, for ever and ever. Amen.

'The everlasting God has in His wisdom foreseen from Eternity the Cross that He now presents to you as a gift from His inmost heart. This Cross He now sends you He has considered with His all-knowing eyes, understood with His Divine Mind, tested with His wise justice, warmed with loving arms and weighed with His own hands to see that it be not one inch too large and not one ounce too heavy for you. He has blessed it with His holy Name, anointed it with His grace, perfumed it with His consolations, taken one last glance at you and your courage, and then sent it to you from Heaven: a special greeting from God to you, an alms of the all-merciful love of God.'

St Francis de Sales

– This is not wisdom only for near the close of life; we have His Cross to carry every day that we live. Every day we have so much to thank Him for, and also so much to offer up to Him in reparation for sin. (Turn again to the question on the back cover.)

'Grant, O Lord, that we see ourselves as Thou seest us and never flinch from doing Thy Will. Forgive us our sins and keep our minds only on Thee and not on the fleeting moments so prized by a secular world. Amen.'

Recall, finally, that it is not 'I am who I am, I love God and my neighbour, and I do what I think is best'. No, we are whom our loving God created us to be and sustains. My life is about obedience to commands which frequently run counter to my own inclination, about recognition of the sinfulness of my own nature. It was for my life that Christ was obedient, obedient unto death, death on the Cross.

After His Resurrection Jesus spoke to the eleven in Galilee: 'All authority in heaven and on earth has been given to Me; you, therefore, must go out, making disciples of all nations, and baptizing them in the name of the Father, and of the Son, and of the Holy Ghost, teaching them to observe all the commandments which I have given you. And behold I am with you all through the days that are coming, until the consummation of the world' (Matthew 28:18–20, in the Ronald Knox translation, 1945).

Will you choose to be His disciple and teach His Word to your neighbour, whom you love as yourself, so that Jesus Christ will be with you always on your journey of life?

Listen to St. Thomas Aquinas again:

'In cases of necessity where faith is in danger, everyone is bound to proclaim his faith, either to give a good example and encouragement to the rest of the faithful, or to check the attacks of unbelievers'. (*Summa Theologica*)

In the words of a traditional Gaelic blessing:
May the road rise with us, the wind be always at our back, and may the Lord hold us in the hollow of His hand.'

A POSTSCRIPT, added in October 2006

'Most people do more willingly listen to the world than to God; they sooner follow the desires of their own flesh than God's good pleasure.'   St. Thomas à Kempis

Please God, when I die, I want to wake up with Thee.

Epilogue

To conclude, here is a quotation from the pen of a literary genius which in three lines encapsulates all I have been trying to convey to my readers:

'Will made the world. Will wounded the world. The same divine Will gave to the world for a second time its chance. The same human will can for the last time make its choice.'

The Common Man, G. K. Chesterton

Gilbert Keith Chesterton was born in 1874. A convert at the age of forty-eight, he was a great friend of another outstanding Catholic writer, Hilaire Belloc, who wrote *On the Place of Gilbert Chesterton in English Letters* four years after his death in 1940. The works of both writers are a library in themselves. Look for them, including Chesterton's Father Brown detective series; enjoy them and benefit hugely from them.

An endearing G. K. trait was his absent-mindedness. He once sent this telegram to his wife: 'Am in Market Harborough. Where ought I to be?' He never forgot, however, nor did Belloc, that God had to guide all he thought and did, an example to us all.

Walter de la Mare, Poet Laureate, wrote this epitaph:

'Knight of the Holy Ghost, he goes his way,
Wisdom his motley, Truth his loving jest:
The mills of Satan keep his lance in play,
Pity and innocence his heart at rest.'

Another quotation from a layman sums up the message of my book:

'To reality, men sooner or later return but they will only return to it through suffering, and with humble and contrite hearts.

Blood must be shed and humiliation endured before they again understand that sacrifice, not satisfied desire, is the way to fulfilment; that work, not money, is the measure of achievement; that fruitfulness, not pleasure, is the end of passion; that strength, not stratagems, is the basis of authority; that faith, not knowledge, is the way to understanding; that duty, not indulgence, is the path they must tread, and their common humanity, not their unique ego, what will hearten them to tread it.'

Malcolm Muggeridge in *Time and Tide*, 1935

A controversial but brilliant British writer and broadcaster whose life (1909-90) was a quest for absolute truth, an honest man with the courage to tell the truth as he saw it no matter whom he upset, he found formal religion by the end of the sixties and, hugely impressed by Mother Teresa, of whom he made a television film, he became a Catholic in 1988. He was 'a prophet not without honour save in his own country', where he became known affectionately as 'St Mugg' Married for sixty-three years, he had four children, (cf. André Frossard, page 71. Also see Book List)

A closing prayer:

'Behold, now is the acceptable time; behold, now is the time of salvation' (2 Corinthians 6:2). Attentive to my so oft repaired cloak I should and will wake up to God: in me, in my neighbour and in everything that is our world, and in all that I say and do. Holy Mary, Mother of Jesus and of His Church, pray for me now and at the hour of my death.

Gloria et gratia, Patri, et Filio, et Spiritui Sancto, sicut erat in principio, et nunc, et semper, et in saecula saeculorum.

Amen

Book List

How many pills and potions do we have in our medicine cupboard against the pains and ills which might afflict our bodies, or to cure ailments which do not seem to require a visit to the doctor? In contrast, how many resources close at hand do we have for the health of our much more important souls and our spiritual life, resources for the treatment of failings, errors and omissions which do not warrant a visit to our confessor? Most of us have a doctor, but do we have a confessor? Do we have books to which we can refer to strengthen or heal our spirits, to help us resolve doubts and to enliven our faith (see Chapter 13)?

Suggested for daily readings and to check my references:
The Holy Bible

I have used the Revised Standard Version (Holman Bible Publishers, Nashville, USA, 1982; Illustrated Verse Reference edition – Concordance) but do go to a bookshop and look for some of your favourite passages in different translations and choose the one you like best. Be sure it has the approval of the Catholic hierarchy. Since reading the Bible is a daunting task, it is useful to have some expert guidance on how to make it less so. 'The Old and New Testaments', writes Alan Hayward, 'are like two halves of a jigsaw puzzle. It is impossible to make complete sense of one without the other. For this reason Old and New Testament readings are interspersed in the list below:

The Gospel of Mark
Genesis
Exodus (chapters 1–24)

Joshua (chapters 1–10 and 24), Judges and Ruth
The Acts of the Apostles
I and II Samuel
The Gospel of Matthew
I and II Kings
Paul's Epistles to Timothy, Titus and Philemon
Ezra, Nehemiah and Esther
The Epistles of James, Peter and John
Proverbs
Paul's Epistles to the Corinthians and the Philippians
Isaiah
The Gospel of John
Jonah and Malachi.'

Quoted from *God's Truth* by Alan Hayward, Marshall, Morgan & Scott (paperback), 1977.

– There are three books which might be an alternative to – or a lead-in for – the Bible:

The Coming of the Kingdom (a short Bible – illustrated), Geoffrey Chapman, London, 1966

New World (the heart of the New Testament in plain English), Alan T. Dale, Oxford University Press, 1967

The Living New Testament (The New Testament paraphrased in everyday language for everyone), Kenneth Taylor, Hodder & Stoughton, London, 1969

Daily reading continued:

Pray the Rosary Daily
The Imitation of Christ, Thomas à Kempis, various
Butler's *Lives of the Saints,* original edition
The Treasury of Catholic Wisdom, Fr John A. Hardon SJ, Ignatius Press, USA, 1994

The Sinner's Guide, Venerable Louis of Granada (1504–88), Tan Books, USA, 1985

For interesting and/or instructive light reading:

Where We Got the Bible, Henry Graham, Tan Books, USA, 1977

The Complete Catholic Handbook, Britons Catholic Library, 1987

The Religion of the Plain Man, Robert Hugh Benson, Burns & Oates, 1906; Servant, 1982 (revised)

Theology for Beginners, F. J. Sheed, Sheed & Ward, London, 1958

The Screwtape Letters, C. S. Lewis, Fount, UK, 1982, 1993

Vintage [Malcolm] *Muggeridge, Religion and Society,* (Ed.) Geoffrey Barlow, Angel Press, Chichester, West Sussex, 1989

Fatima in Lucia's Own Words, Lucia Santos, USA, 1989

Fatima's Message for Our Times, Mgr J. A. Cirrincone, Tan, USA, 1990

The Snakebite Letters, Peter Kreeft, Ignatius Press, USA, UK, 1993

The Desolate City, Anne Roche Muggeridge, Harper & Rowe, USA, 1990

God's Truth, Alan Hayward, Marshall, Morgan & Scott, Lakeland, UK, 1977

Rafael, Cardinal Merry del Val, Marie Cecilia Buehrle, Sands, UK, 1957

Crossing the Threshold of Hope, His Holiness John Paul II, Jonathan Cape, UK, 1994

Where is God when it Hurts, Philip Yancey, Pickering & Inglis, London, 1979

The Prophet, Kahlil Gibran, William Heinemann, London, 1994
– I have a small notebook in which to make notes and record striking sentences or short passages. At the back, I make a list of recommended further reading and books which might be of interest to me. There is no more important a reading list.

For more serious reading:
Catechism of the Catholic Church, Geoffrey Chapman, London, 1994 (You should own a copy.)
A Catechism of Christian Doctrine (the old Penny Catechism) Catholic Truth Society, 1979 (Buy this and learn it by heart.)
Compendium of the Catechism of the Catholic Church, Catholic Truth Society, London 2006.
The New Morality, Arnold Lunn & Garth Lean, Blandford Press, London, 1964
Death: the Glorious Adventure, David L. Greenstock, Burns & Oates, London, 1956
Hell and its Torments, St Robert Bellarmine, Tan Books, USA, 1990
Confession: A Little Book for the Reluctant Mgr L. G. de Segur, Tan Books, USA, 1989
To Know Jesus Christ, F. J. Sheed, Sheed & Ward, London, 1983
Society and Sanity, F. J. Sheed, Sheed & Ward, London, 1983
Humanae Vitae, Pope Paul VI, CTS, London
Sex Instruction in the Home, Helen M. Davies MD, Real Press for the Association of Catholic Women, Surbiton, England, 1993
Preparing for Marriage, John Marshall, Darton, Longman & Todd Ltd, UK, 1966
Parents, Children and God, Anthony Bullen, Fontana/Collins, UK, 1972

Creation Rediscovered, G. J. Keane, Author, Australia, 1991
The Facts of Life, Richard Milton, Corgi Books, London, 1993
The War Against Population, Jacqueline Kasun, Ignatius Press, NY Greenhill, 1987
The Rhine Flows into the Tiber: A History of Vatican II, Fr Ralph M. Wiltgen SVD, Tan Books, USA, 1988
The Devastated Vineyard, Dietrich von Hildebrand, Roman Catholic Books, NY, 1985
The Oxford History of Christianity, ed. John Manners, Oxford University Press, 1993
The Bible as History, Werner Keller (trans.), Reprint Society, SPCK, 1991
The Living World of the Old Testament, Bernard W. Anderson, Longman, London, 1966
Who Moved the Stone? Frank Morrison, Faber, London, 1944

Advanced study:
The Man and the Woman, Evoy and O'Keefe, Sheed & Ward, NY, 1968
Theology and Sanity, F. J. Sheed, Sheed & Ward, London, 1947
Teilhardism and the New Religion, Wolfgang Smith, Tan Books, USA, 1988
Gaudium et Spes, CTS, London
The Documents of Vatican II, Walter M. Abbott SJ, Geoffrey Chapman, London, 1967
Sex and Culture, Dr J. R. Unwin, Oxford University Press, 1934
Veritatis Splendor, Pope John Paul II, CTS, London
Evangelium Vitae, Pope John Paul II, CTS, London
Salvifici Doloris, Pope John Paul II, CTS, London
The Reform of the Roman Liturgy, Mgr Klaus Gamber (translated), Una Voce Press, USA, 1993

– Most of these books should be readily available, or by order, in religious bookshops. Second-hand they may be

obtained by post from: John Bevan at Romans Halt, Mildenhall, Marlborough, Wilts. SN8 2LX Tel.01672 519817
– In any event, all the books on the List can be applied for in public libraries on payment of a small charge. Start a 'library apostolate' by getting these books into circulation for other readers.
– Many of the titles listed are not what might be your image of religious books, and will repay a browsing interest in a bookshop so that you first get a taste of them.

Internet resources :
Since this book was written, a new source of information has become available to everyone with a computer. Here are some web sites likely to prove of great interest:

www.proecclesia.com	Supporting the teachings of the Catholic Church
www.catholic.com	Catholic answers
www.ignaisinsight.com	A journal of culture, theology and news
www.vatican.va	
www.churchinhistory.org	
www.cts-online.org.com	Catholic Truth Society: books and resources
www.catholicschool.org.uk	To obtain Catholic educational materials

✠

Blessing of St Clare, the sister of St Francis of Assisi:
'May the Lord bless you and keep you,
May He show His face to you, and be merciful to you,
May He turn His countenance to you and give you His peace.
May the Lord be with you always, and, wherever you are,
May you be with Him always.
Amen.'

Thank you for reading my little book, and I should welcome your comments and suggestions, or any of your questions, which, please, you may send to me, c/o the Publisher.

May, the month of Our Blessed Lady, 1995
J. M. REID

OMEGA Work-out
(Open My Ears to God Again Work-out)

This comprises a series of **get-togethers** of, say, up to twelve Faithful who will use this book as a manual. Proceeding chapter by chapter, twelve monthly meetings of two to three hours would complete the Work-out in a year. It is likely that even two or three meetings, which could be held weekly or fortnightly would be sufficient to have an impact and result in a start on a personal effort of the envisaged active renewal and witness.

The idea is to select several chapters for each meeting and **to discuss** the particular teaching in each, and any doubts raised, with the aim of strengthening knowledge and understanding of the former and resolving the latter.

To be done effectively, it is essential that there be **preparatory study** (revision) of the true teaching of the Church seeking the guidance of the Holy Spirit.

Such study will not be fruitful without additional **praying**. There are over fifty prayers in the book; some may prove attractive additions to each person's current daily prayer habits but others suggested by participants can be selected.

An essential contribution will be regular attendance at **Holy Mass** at least every Sunday and to receive the Body of Jesus Christ. In particular, a commitment will be requested: to seek God's forgiveness and His grace regularly at short (monthly?) intervals, if possible from a chosen confessor who can also offer advice on contentious issues of conscience.

The objective is to extend and deepen knowledge and understanding of the true teaching of the Church so that the Faithful can witness their Faith and, as urged by Vatican II, **be active Disciples of Christ**.

Each get-together would benefit from the leadership of a trained pastor who could start by offering Mass. However, as the book emphasises, diligent DIY in the form of recourse to the two reference books every Catholic home should have, namely the Catechism of the Catholic Church, or the Compendium of the Catechism of the Catholic Church and the Bible, or at least the New Testament, would ensure the availability of the necessary material for informed discussion. Aided by a leader chosen for each meeting to nudge the proceedings along, measured, steady progress towards the objective can be confidently expected **under the aegis of the Holy Spirit.**

The OMEGA Work-out can even be undertaken alone by a resolute individual. Pray to St. Athanasius of Alexandria (296-373), staunch, solo defender of the Nicene creed.

Why use 'Wake up to God'? Its purpose is that of a 'primer' in the four meanings of that word (page 7 para. 1). Also, unusually it offers many prayers as well as a presentation of the true teaching of the Church. Awarded an *Imprimatur* and *Nihil obstat*, the book roughly follows the classical pattern of the Catechism; its content is orthodox, drawn from authentic, quoted sources; it has a proven record, based on scores of letters from readers, lay and religious, of being a stimulating tonic as well as a guide and comfort. It has shortcomings but these will emerge in the discussions and corrections can be noted.

In Britain it is evident - supported by official figures - that there is a serious decline in the attention the Faithful give to their religion: in particular, to Sunday Mass and, especially, to the Sacrament of Reconciliation (Confession); to improving our knowledge and understanding of the true teaching of the Catholic Church, especially with regard to morals and, in particular, contraception; to religious reading and to our prayer life. The Work-out addresses all these issues so as to re-awaken us to God in and with us, and that we know how to serve Him with love and obedience in this life in order to be happy with Him for ever in the next.

1998   J.M.R

Table of Contents

Contents/Index	Prayers	Page Nos.
Preface	Opening Prayer	7
1 Purpose	'Come, Holy Spirit'	11
2 Is There a God?	'I believe'	14
3 Creation, Fall and Redemption	Prayer of Thanksgiving	16
4 What about Evolution?	A French translation	19
5 Prayer	'Lord, I shall be very busy'	23
6 The Bible	'Holy Michael Archangel'	27
7 Why Did God Make Me?	'I consecrate to Thee'	30
8 Is Jesus the Son of God?	Stations of the Cross	34
9 His Church	'Salve Regina'	36
10 Our Mortality	The 'Confiteor'	40
11 Bad Popes	Prayer to St Peter	43
12 Judgment at Death	H. J. Kaiser's Prayer	47
13 Eternity	'Homesick for Heaven'	50
14 'Thy Will be Done'	Ave Maria	52
15 Why a Church?	St Thomas Aquinas	54
16 My Guardian Angel	'O Angel of God'	58
17 Satan	Repeat of 'Holy Michael'	60
18 Sin	Self-examination and meditation	62
19 Redeemed	'God, be merciful to me'	65
20 Our Purpose – Again	Pentecost Sequence	67
21 The Creed	The Apostles' Creed	70
22 The Two Great Commandments	Three prayers	72
23 Worshipping God	Prayer of Cardinal Cushing	75
24 Mortal Sin	Act of Contrition	78

Table of Contents

Contents/Index		Prayers	Page Nos.
25	Penance and Fasting	Psalm 22:16–17	82
26	Purgatory	Prayer for the Holy Souls	84
27	The Sacraments	'Pater Noster'	86
28	Holy Matrimony	For the Institution of Marriage	88
29	Male and Female	For Chastity	91
30	Sexual Conduct	Proverbs 2:1–15	95
31	Sexual Morality	'Dear Lord and Father'	101
32	Contraception	'Memorare'	107
33	Virginity, Chastity and Celibacy	A Quartet of Intercession	111
34	The Priesthood	Prayer for Vocations	114
35	The Family is Fundamental	The Rosary	117
36	Killing and Stealing	Cardinal Newman	121
37	Abortion	Psalm 12	125
38	Live in Truth	St Thomas à Kempis	129
39	The Tenth Commandment	The Beatitudes	131
40	Priorities	'Most Sacred Heart of Jesus'	133
41	Conscience	Cardinal Merry del Val	136
42	Grow in Study	'Our Lady of Fatima'	139
43	Grow in Prayer and Love	The Last Gospel	142
44	Trompe-l'oeil	A Psalm of Islam	145
45	Personal Freedom	St Martin de Porres	148
46	The Journey of Life	St Francis de Sales	151
	Epilogue	'Closing Prayer'	157
	Book List	Blessing of St Clare	159
	OMEGA Work-out		165